Dre...

For thousa... dered about dr... purpose to them... ...ply serve as casual entertainment for a tired body? Many dreams do give us messages to our benefit. Some dreams are even precognitive—telling us what is going to happen in the future. A dream can have particular meaning for one person yet a similar dream can have a totally different meaning for someone else. How can this be?

Secrets of Gypsy Dream Reading can answer these questions and more. This book is the product of generations of observations undertaken by a people who have always lived close to the Mysteries of Life—the Gypsies.

If you wonder about the meaning of dreams, if you want to learn *how* to interpret, then this book is for you. Not only does it give a full and comprehensive listing of the meanings of hundreds of dream symbols, but it also explains how the Gypsies relate dreams to the individual and how they thereby interpret accurately.

In addition, this book reveals the secrets of dreaming the future. Learn how to profit from your dreams. No longer need dreams be mere "nighttime movies" . . . they can be tools for a more rewarding and fulfilling life.

About the Author

Ray Buckland's grandfather was the first of the Buckland Gypsies to give up traveling the roads in waggons and to settle in a permanent house. From his earliest years Ray remembers listening to his father's and grandfather's tales of Romani life, and watching his grandmother read cards and tell fortunes. This upbringing instilled in him a deep respect for the Old Ways. From his teens, Ray Buckland started his own serious studies of the Old Knowledge, and later, came to write about it in a number of best-selling books. "Buckland" is a well-known name among English Gypsies, and Ray Buckland has become a well-known author of books on practical magic. He is today regarded as one of the leading authorities on witchcraft, voodoo and the supernatural.

To Write to the Author

We cannot guarantee that every letter written to the author can be answered, but all will be forwarded. Both the author and the publisher appreciate hearing from readers, learning of your enjoyment and benefit from this book. Llewellyn also publishes a bi-monthly news magazine with news and reviews of practical esoteric studies and articles helpful to the student, and some readers' questions and comments to the author may be answered through this magazine's columns if permission to do so is included in the original letter. The author sometimes participates in seminars and workshops, and dates and places are announced in *The Llewellyn New Times*. To write to the author, or to ask a question, write to:

Raymond Buckland
c/o THE LLEWELLYN NEW TIMES
P.O. Box 64383-086, St. Paul, MN 55164-0383, U.S.A.
Please enclose a self-addressed, stamped envelope for reply,
or $1.00 to cover costs.

Llewellyn's New Age Series

Secrets of Gypsy Dream Reading

Raymond Buckland

1990
Llewellyn Publications
St. Paul, Minnesota, 55164-0383, U.S.A.

Cover art by Victoria Poyser Lisi

Library of Congress Cataloging-in-Publication Data

Buckland, Raymond, 1934-
    Secrets of Gypsy dream reading / by
Raymond Buckland
        p.   cm. — (Llewellyn's new age series)
    ISBN 0-87542-086-9
    1. Dreams. 2. Gypsies—England—Folklore. 3. Folklore—England. I. Title. II. Series.
BF1091.B89   1990   90-39288
135'.3' 08991497—dc20   CIP

90 91 92 93   10 9 8 7 6 5 4 3 2 1

Llewellyn Publications
A Division of Llewellyn Worldwide, Ltd.
P.O. Box 64383, St. Paul, MN 55164-0383

ABOUT LLEWELLYN'S NEW AGE SERIES

The "New Age"—it's a phrase we use, but what does it mean? Does it mean that we are entering the Aquarian Age? Does it mean that a new Messiah is coming to correct all that is wrong and make the Earth into a Garden? Probably not—but the idea of a *major change* is there, combined with awareness that the Earth *can* be a Garden; that war, crime, poverty, disease, etc., are not necessary "evils."

Optimists, dreamers, scientists . . . nearly all of us believe in a "better tomorrow," and that somehow we can do things now that will make for a better future life for ourselves and for coming generations.

In one sense, we all know there's nothing new under the Heavens, and in another sense that every day makes a new world. The difference is in our consciousness. And this is what the New Age is all about: it's a major change in consciousness found within each of us as we learn to bring forth and manifest powers that Humanity has always potentially had.

You still have to learn the "rules" for developing and applying these powers, but it is more like "relearning" than a *new* learning, because with the New Age it is as if the basis for these had become genetic.

Other Books by Raymond Buckland

Practical Candleburning Rituals
Witchcraft from the Inside
Witchcraft . . . the Religion
A Pocket Guide to the Supernatural
Witchcraft Ancient and Modern
Here Is the Occult
The Tree: Complete Book of Saxon Witchcraft
The Magic of Chant-O-Matics
Anatomy of the Occult
Practical Color Magick
Buckland's Complete Book of Witchcraft
Secrets of Gypsy Fortunetelling
Buckland's Gypsy Fortunetelling Deck
Secrets of Gypsy Love Magick

With Hereward Carrington

Amazing Secrets of the Psychic World

Under the Pseudonym "Tony Earll"

Mu Revealed

Forthcoming by Raymond Buckland

Scottish Witchcraft
Gypsy Shamanism
A Witch's Potpourri

CONTENTS

Gypsies and Dreaming 1

Symbolism in Dreams 7

Universal Symbolism 13

Dream Interpretation 173

Lucid Dreaming 179

Prophetic Dreams 185

Dreaming for Profit 193

1
Gypsies and Dreaming

Gypsies hold much stock in dreams and are renowned dream interpreters. Although Tunisian and Algerian Romanis are the recognized experts in this field, English Gypsies certainly have practiced dream interpretation for many generations.

In common with all Gypsies, the English travelers maintain that through dreams they are being given secret knowledge that could affect their future, positively or negatively. They believe dreams come from the spirits of ancestors.

In my two previous books on the Rom (*Secrets of Gypsy Fortunetelling* and *Secrets of Gypsy Love Magick*) I relate how people will visit Gypsies, at their encampments, either to have their fortunes told or to learn about performing magick. Dream interpretation is yet another reason for these visits. Many people—country born or city bred, it doesn't seem to matter which—are curious about various "nighttime movies of the mind." Are these nothing more than "movies" for the entertainment of our unconscious selves, or is there some real significance to dreams?

The first thing a knowledgeable Rom will do, when approached on this score, is inquire as to the general health and eating habits of the person. Most of us, Gypsies included, are aware that much dreaming is simply the result of excesses in eating and/or drinking. Charles Bowness, in *Romany Magic* (Samuel Weiser, New York, 1973), says:

> "Apart from those dreams brought on by stomachic derangement there are also those occasioned by some bodily excitation due to a previous pleasant or unpleasant experience. Another cause is tension owing to brooding over some problem or fear of a future event.
>
> "To categorize further, dreams of terror can be due to a slight and temporary disorder of the heart. Similarly, a defect in the lungs can be responsible for a dream of bloodshed. To experience some enormous difficulty in a dream, such as hacking a way through a jungle, or trying to penetrate a wall indicates disorder of the liver. Dreaming of sharp

pains, knife stabs in the back and the like, is because of kidney disorder. If a dream contains some element of hypnotic regularity such as the swinging of a pendulum, then there may well be a tendency to anaemia.

"This is by no means a complete list of the physical causes of dreams, but it will suffice as a general guide."

It is obvious that you cannot simply take *any* dream and say "Oh, yes. That means such-and-such." The question is, then, which dreams *can* be interpreted? The Gypsies say any dream which is especially vivid; one that stays with you long after you wake. Additionally, it should be one that is dreamed when you are in good health and have not overindulged the night before.

An immediate problem, however, is that the unconscious mind does not like to let go. It does not like to leave a dream all nicely cut and dried. Rather, it will embellish, and keep on embellishing. For this reason it is of prime importance to write down every single detail that you remember about a dream *as soon as you wake up*. If you stop for breakfast, or even just a quick cup of coffee, you will find yourself "remembering" other things about the dream ... yet there is no guarantee that these things really were in that dream. As the day progresses, and you keep reflecting on your dream, you will seem to remember more and more about it; you will seem to be filling in the blanks. But these "remembrances" are far more likely to be embellishments that the unconscious mind is now adding to make the dream story more interesting.

Just how "sneaky" the unconscious mind can be at times is detailed by Charles Godfrey Leland (*Gypsy Sorcery and Fortune Telling*, 1891), relating a dream he had once when staying in Germany:

"I thought I was in my bed yet I did not know exactly where I was. I at once perceived the anomaly, and was in great distress to know whether I was awake or in a dream. I seemed to be an invalid. I realized, or knew, that in another bed near mine was a nurse or attendant. I begged her to tell me if I were dreaming, and to awake me if I were. She tried to persuade me that I was in my ordinary life, awake. I was not at all satisfied. I arose and went (out) into the street. There I met with two or three common men. I felt great hesitation in addressing them on such a singular subject, but told them I was in distress because I feared that I was in a dream, and begged them to shake or squeeze my arm. I forget whether they complied, but I went on and met three gentlemen, to whom I made the same request. One at once promptly declared that he remembered me, saying that we had met before in Cincinnati. He pressed my arm, but it had no effect. I began to believe that I was really awake. I returned to the room. I heard a child speaking or murmuring by the nurse. I asked her again to shake my hand. This she did so forcibly that I was now *perfectly* convinced that it was no dream. And the instant it came home to me that it was a reality, there seized me the thrill or feeling of a coming nightmare—and I awoke!"

So the moment he determined that in fact he was *not* dreaming, he woke up . . . proving that he in fact *was* dreaming! Many times we have dreams where we are not sure whether we are dreaming or are, in fact, awake. Sometimes you will seemingly wake up, get up out of bed, get dressed, go out to the kitchen . . . and then suddenly find that you are still lying in bed. This is known as a "false awakening." In such an example you have, in all probability, actually experienced a brief moment of astral projection, which ties in with many dreams.

On the opposite side, there are times when you can be dreaming and fully realize that you *are* asleep and dreaming; you can, in effect, watch your dream—much as a third party—and even direct it. This is known as "lucid dreaming," and I'll talk more about that later in this book.

But to most people it is the mystery of meaning in dreams that intrigues. When you do awaken, and when you remember what you have dreamed, then you want to know what that dream meant. Presuming that you have met the Gypsies' criteria—healthy, with no late evening overindulgences—then we can examine what you experienced.

2
Symbolism in Dreams

Modern science says that we spend anywhere from twenty-five to fifty per cent of our sleeping time in the dream state; we have an average of six dream periods every night and each dream lasts anywhere up to forty minutes. Apparently if we didn't have these dreams we would go crazy. Most of them are from our unconscious mind, trying to get a message across to us for our own well-being. Gypsies believe that these messages come from ancestral spirits. Who is to say they are wrong? That may be what our unconscious mind is—proddings from the spirits. The point is that, if we are being given these messages for our own well-being, it would behoove us to try to understand them; to listen to the spirits. The unconscious, or the spirits, employ symbols with which we are familiar. They present the message using objects that pertain to everyday life, the better that we may understand what is being communicated.

Universal and Personal Symbolism

There are two kinds of symbols that come through to us: *universal* symbols and *personal* symbols.

Suppose you dream about a castle. Now it could well be that you watch a lot of late night television and see many old movies featuring vampires living in castles. From this it could be that you automatically associate castles with evil. You might do this consciously or it might be an unconscious association. Either way, when you think, see, or dream castles, you conceptualize "evil." Yet you could have a very good, close friend who is interested in architecture and considers the castle to be a thing of beauty; the height of the architect's craft. For him or her the association of castles with evil is ridiculous. A third person might have grown up in Europe and actually lived in a castle for a period. He or she considers them neither evil nor beautiful; simply cold, damp, and drafty! So here you have three totally different reactions to castles. Obviously there could be more. These, then, are *personal* interpretations. Any one of these three people, having a dream about a castle, would have to consider this personal association when deciding what the dream meant.

Yet there is also a *universal* symbolism for castles. They are associated with ambition. "Ambition" is the interpretation that would be used by the majority of people when they have no particularly strong, personal feelings about castles. As I say in *Buckland's Complete Book of Witchcraft*, "*Universal Symbolism* includes those things that remain true for all humankind throughout the ages. Included are colors, numbers, form and sexual identity (*i.e.* male and female) They come from the super-consciousness and therefore are timeless." I go on to give the example of transportation: "(It is) the universal symbol of spiritual advancement. As material technology has advanced, the application of symbology has kept pace. So transportation may take one of the modern forms of conveyance, such as rockets, planes, steamships, trains or automobiles, or one of the timeless modes of riding on the back of an animal or walking."

When you set out to interpret your dreams, therefore, you need to look at each and every one of the symbols and decide what it means *for you*. If something has a special, *personal* meaning, then go with that. If it has no special meaning, interpret according to the universal symbolism. It stands to reason, however, that in the unlikely event of two people having identical dreams they would not mean the same thing for both people, just as in card reading no two cards mean the same thing for two people. When a Gypsy interprets your dream, he or she will ask a lot of questions in order to find out the personal significance of each and every symbol.

In the listing of dream symbols which follows, I can, of course, only give the universal meaning. What you have to do is to see whether that meaning fits for you or whether you have a stronger, more personal feeling with regard to that symbol; a feeling/interpretation that is far more significant for you. As Carl Jung said: "No dream symbol can be separated from the individual who dreams it."

After the listing of symbols I will discuss interpretation in greater detail. I will also talk about the prophetic dream—that which tells you something about the future—and how to decide, ahead of time, what you *want* to dream . . . even if it's the winner of tomorrow's horse race!

3
Universal Symbolism

ABBEY/MONASTERY Sanctuary; temporary safety. To dream that you are in an abbey is confirmation that you are safe and have no cause to worry needlessly, though this safety may only be temporary. To come upon an abbey unexpectedly is a sign that there is help around the corner. Apply this to any worries you may have and look at the other symbols in the dream and how they relate to this.

ABBOT Someone has power/authority over you; can make you do things you don't necessarily want to do. There is a restriction in your life. You may not be aware of this consciously so examine your situation, and those with whom you are in close contact.

ABORTION You will not succeed in the project you are presently working on. Better make alternate plans.

ABYSS Exercise caution, there is possible danger ahead. An abyss can also mean an invitation—to adventure, opportunity . . . or danger.

ACCEPTANCE For some reason this seems to work with opposite meaning. Slow and laborious progress before final acceptance in a dream indicates quick success to come, while easy acceptance indicates trouble ahead. Acceptance can be shown in many ways. Perhaps, in your dream, you propose to a young lady and she accepts. An easy, almost immediate acceptance would forebode trouble ahead. Gypsies say that for a young woman to dream that she has accepted her lover's marriage proposal is a sign that there will be an unexpected delay in their wedding plans.

ACCIDENT Any sort of accident—car, household, job-related—is indicative of self-criticism. You have done something of which you are not proud. Examine your recent actions and see if you can undo the problem.

ACCORDION A popular Gypsy instrument.

To dream of playing an accordion indicates that you are having to work hard to achieve your desires. Yet if you dream that you are having a wonderful, happy time playing it—perhaps with lots of people dancing to the music—then it means you are enjoying your job and are happiest when working.

ACCUSATION Torment; distress; self-doubt. If, in your dream, someone points the finger at you, then it is really *you* doubting yourself.

ACE To dream of playing cards, or handling cards, and especially noticing one of the aces, means that you will be a key figure in a love affair (ace of hearts), a law suit (ace of clubs), a legacy (ace of diamonds), or a scandal (ace of spades).

ACORN(S) The Gypsies say that dreaming of acorns means your plans will take a while to come to fruition, but when they do they will far exceed your greatest hopes.

ACTOR/ACTRESS If you see yourself as an actor/actress then you will be the bearer of good news. If you meet with, or watch (as part of an audience), actor(s) then you will be the recipient of good news.

ADDRESS To write out an address on a letter indicates that you have found direction; you now know where you are going. You have set your goals and can move forward.

ADMIRAL See *Colonel / Military Officer*.

ADORATION To be the object of adoration in a dream indicates that you can be a big flirt. You should beware of becoming conceited. If, in the dream, you are the one who is doing the adoring, beware of being misled; exercise caution.

AIRPLANE In general, transportation symbolizes spiritual advancement. Examine the rest of the dream and see if it does, indeed, tie in with that interpretation. If so, this modern, rapid form of transportation needs to be handled carefully lest it crash. If not, then it may simply indicate rapid advancement with opportunity for self-expression, especially if you are the pilot of the plane.

AISLE A division; a parting. To dream of the aisle of a church often indicates a forthcoming disagreement between two factions of a family. Gypsy families will always ensure that they are all together on one side of a church aisle, rather than some on one side and some on the other.

ALARM CLOCK You are afraid of growing old. You have many plans and wonder if you'll ever have time to implement them all. (See also *Clock*.)

ALDER An alder tree is an omen of happiness and impending good news.

ALLIGATOR See *Crocodile*.

ALMS To give, or to receive, alms indicates that your business will be successful and you will become wealthy.

ALTAR Prosperity; peace. A center point; a focal point.

AMBULANCE To see an ambulance indicates that you should exercise caution or you may have an accident. To be riding in an ambulance means you have made a grave error. Look back over your recent actions and see if you can spot the error and rectify it.

ANCHOR Foundation; security. You have some base; some foundation upon which to build. You are secure, but it should be kept in mind that an anchor can sometimes hold you back when you want to be moving.

ANGEL Coming news that may or may not be good. It may well be that what at first glance appears to be good news is, on closer examination, bad news—and vice versa.

ANIMALS See separate headings for individual animals.

ANTS If you dream of ants on your clothing, or coming into your home, you will have petty annoyances. To watch ants is to indulge in activity; usually a lot of small jobs. An anthill is a sign of avoidance of work.

ANVIL See *Blacksmith*.

APE/MONKEY Symbolizes deceit. Beware of business associates trying to cheat you.

Judge friends by their actions rather than by their words.

APPLE An old Gypsy tenet states: "Should a girl wish to dream of her future husband, it is necessary for her to obtain an apple from a widow on Saint Andrew's Eve. She must not give thanks for receipt of the apple, and should eat half of it before midnight, and the other half after midnight. Her future lover will then be revealed whilst she is asleep." (Also see *Fruits*.)

APRICOTS See *Fruits*.

APRON To be wearing an apron means you

will be taking orders from another, but getting satisfaction from it.

ARCHBISHOP See *Abbot*.

ARCHERY See *Arrow*.

ARM If it is an arm offered to you, it can mean assistance. If you find an arm barring your way, exercise caution; carefully think through any plans you have for the future. A broken arm means the death of a relative (Gypsies say the left arm represents a female and the right arm a male). An arm that is excessively hairy indicates money coming to you.

ARMCHAIR Whether the armchair is empty or whether you are sitting in it doesn't matter. It means that you are firmly established in your present position and no one can move you out of it without your permission.

ARMOR To dream of being dressed in a suit of armor means you feel very secure, especially regarding financial matters. To see a suit of armor on display means you are worried about lack of security.

ARMY Armed men are generally a good sign.

If it is a marching army then great things are afoot, with many major forces at work, usually in your favor. A battle indicates a scandal.

ARREST If you are arrested in your dreams it means you are taking unnecessary chances. Be more cautious.

ARROW Usually a bad omen. An arrow shot by someone else and hitting you means there will be bad gossip about you. If you shoot an arrow in the air, your lover is unfaithful. (See, also, *Shooting*.)

ASHES To dream of ashes in a stove, or fireplace, or to dream of clearing ashes, means you feel the work you are doing is beneath you. You are dissatisfied with your job.

ASS/DONKEY A quarrel between friends. If it is trotting it means disappointed hopes; if running, disaster. But to be given a donkey or an ass is a sign of business success. To be thrown off the back of one, or be kicked by one, means a quarrel with your lover. If you hear an ass bray, it is great scandal. A heavily laden donkey indicates imminent good fortune.

ASSASSIN Relief from unpleasant circumstances. Final gratification.

AUCTION To be at an auction means you will be getting an unexpected raise in pay. To be the auctioneer means you will have to work hard to earn the raise.

AUNT See *Uncle/Aunt*.

AUTOMOBILE Another symbol of spiritual advancement. Note the speed at which it is traveling . . . or is it standing still? If going uphill, obviously you are really having to work at your progress. A breakdown indicates that you need to reassess your beliefs and practices.

AXE To be wielding an axe means you are respected by others, though more for your position than for your abilities.

BABY/CHILD To dream of a sleeping baby, or small child, means you have a shy, trusting nature. A baby crawling about means you will need to think quickly and make quick decisions. A crying child means you will have a number of small problems to resolve. To breast-feed a baby, or see a baby being breast-fed, means you must beware of confiding in people who are not very close friends.

BACHELOR A man dreaming that he is a bachelor should be cautious in his dealing with women. But according to an old Gypsy woman in Kent, when a woman dreams of a bachelor it is an indication that her lover is fickle.

BACK DOOR There is an unexpected solution to a problem you have. You should search for it; it may be well hidden but it is there.

BACON To slice bacon indicates the coming death of a loved one. To eat bacon means triumph over enemies. If you are smoking, or curing, bacon someone close to you will become ill.

BADGER A badger is a sign of wisdom and sagacity.

BAGPIPES To see and/or hear bagpipes

being played means that help is coming to you from an unexpected source. Scottish Gypsies put great store by this dream symbol.

BAILIFF/SHERIFF If you see a sheriff arrest someone it means there will be arguing within your family. A sheriff coming to take your possessions means you will be facing a lawsuit, but that you will be successful in it.

BAKER/BAKERY Gain; increase. This could be financial gain or it could be increase in the size of your family—a child! According to the Gypsies, it is more likely to be the latter if someone hands you a loaf of bread. Overall, anything to do with a bakery symbolizes joy. (See also *Bread* and *Meeting*.)

BALL Something difficult to hold on to. If it is rolling away from you, then you must work harder to get ahead. If it is rolling towards you, then you can sit back and reap your just reward.

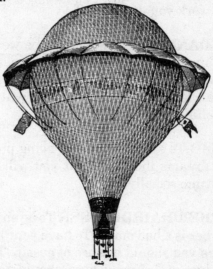

BALLOON It seems solid but, in reality, it is just full of air! Don't be distracted by bright colors. Examine any personal or business offers you receive to make sure they are sound. However, a hot-air balloon—whether you are ascending in one or just watching one go up—is always indicative of financial gain.

BALLROOM/DANCING A ballroom filled with dancers indicates a happy family life. An empty ballroom shows a longing for company and/or family. Intricate dancing symbolizes ability to do well in anything you try. To see others dancing means you will get pleasure from someone else's good fortune. To be dancing yourself means you will get pleasure from work you do yourself.

BANDANNA For a woman to be wearing a bandanna, or *diklo*, over her hair means she will soon be married. For an already-married woman to dream this means she will have a love affair.

BANJO To see/hear a banjo being played in your dreams indicates that you will have a good time socially.

BARBER/HAIRDRESSER To be shaved by a barber is a bad omen. To have your hair cut means you should beware of gossip. To have your hair styled means you should pay more attention to your appearance.

BARE/NAKED If you suddenly become naked, it means you will get a surprise, which could be good or bad. If you are the only person who is naked in a group, it is a warning of scandal to come. If all are naked, it is a sign of warmth, joy, and friendliness.

BARLEY Good fortune.

BARN The Gypsies say that to dream of a full barn means you will never go hungry again. But an empty barn indicates a life of sadness and want. A barn on fire indicates that you could lose all that you have.

BARREL Similar to a barn in that a full barrel indicates plenty and an empty one indicates want. If you are pounding a bung into a barrel then you need to secure what you have.

BARTENDER If you are the bartender, you will be mixing with company that is beneath you. If you are being served by a bartender, you should beware of any advice freely offered. Enjoying company at a bar, you are in need of good companionship.

BASEMENT See *Cellar*.

BASIN A basin of cold water indicates the need to be closer to the family; a need for more warmth between you. A basin of warm water shows that you are loving and caring. A basin of dirty water means there will be family quarrels.

BASKET If you are carrying a full basket you will be offered a better paying job. If the basket is empty you will lose your present job.

BAT A bat flying around means that all your small problems will be cleared up very quickly and easily. If the bat is at rest, hanging upside-down, then what seem like small problems now may later develop into big ones.

BATH To dream of filling a bath with water is a warning against throwing your money down the drain. If you are taking a bath, you are in need of a vacation. If you are in a bath with other people (or a sauna, or hot tub) you should be cautious of business dealings. If you are bathing in dirty water, people are going to gossip.

BATTLEFIELD See *Army*.

BAYONET A symbol for caution. If you stab someone with a bayonet, be careful in your dealings with the opposite sex. If you are stabbed with a bayonet, you will suffer financial loss.

BEAR Great hidden strength. If you kill a bear, you will overcome seemingly insur-mountable odds. If you are chased by a bear, you will have many business problems and have to deal with unpleasant people. If you track/hunt a bear, you will gain status and be greatly respected.

BEARD Dreaming that you wear a beard, when in fact you don't, means that you are very much an individualist and don't care too much about what others think of you.

BEAUTIFUL WOMAN Success in love and/or business. Recognition for your efforts.

BED A neatly made bed means security. An unmade bed means secrets will be discovered. If you are in bed, alone, it indicates loneliness. In bed with someone of the same sex means you will have to apologize for your actions. In bed with someone of the opposite sex, you will have to make a big decision. If you are in a bed that is outdoors, or the bed is empty but outdoors, there is the opportunity to earn a great deal of money.

BEE Profit; gain. If the bees fly away you will be rid of your worries. To be stung by a bee means you will be severely reprimanded.

BEEHIVE Success in business. If you knock over the hive, you will be in for a lawsuit.

BEGGAR Opportunities. To give, freely, to the beggar means you will be making great gains and having tremendous opportunities. To ignore a beggar is to miss out on what could bring you big success. (See also *Meeting*.)

BELLOWS You will be having company. If you are pumping the bellows it means that the company will cause a lot of work for you.

BELLS Gypsies believe that bells generally signify misfortune. A single, tolling bell is a sign of approaching death, or of serious illness. A peal of bells, however, is a sign of coming celebration. A persistent doorbell is an alarm . . . you should be on your guard.

BENCH To dream of sitting on a bench is a warning not to speak too openly about your private affairs with people you don't know very well.

BICYCLE To dream of riding a bicycle means that you are becoming automatic in the work you do. You need to step back and look at the whole picture, giving yourself inspiration to become more creative.

BILLIARDS/POOL To see an empty billiard or pool table means you will be lucky in love. To play the game means that someone is going to be lying to you, or you to them.

BIRDS Birds, in general, mean success. Flying birds indicate a prospective journey. To have a bird land on your hand, arm, or head means an unexpected love is coming into your life. To kill a bird, or find a dead bird, is an ill omen. Gypsies in various parts of England have different ideas about dreams concerning specific birds. Following are a few of those ideas.

Blackbird A need for caution. Examine all business matters carefully.

Canary Death of a friend. A sudden departure. A flying canary means temporary sickness.

Crow You will be disappointed in an expectation and will have to make do with what you have.

Dove Fidelity in love; happiness at home. A flock of doves means an abundance of love and happiness. Two doves together means reconciliation.

Eagle A soaring eagle indicates great business success.

Falcon/Hawk A soaring falcon or hawk, as with an eagle, means business success. A swooping falcon or hawk means success in a legal matter. To carry the bird on your arm and/or release it, indicates branching out, embracing new associates either in your business or personal life.

Lark A short vacation, with fun and relaxation.

Nightingale To hear a nightingale sing is to be assured of happiness.

Owl You must give great thought to a coming problem, rather than making a snap decision. If the owl flies away, you will find the problem is not as big as it seems. To hear an owl hoot is to be warned of coming problems.

Parrot Beware of slander. Don't listen to gossip.

Peacock To dream of a peacock is a sign of popularity, but beware of pride and vanity. If it is a peacock which suddenly spreads its tail, beware of ostentation. To hear a peacock scream means there is an approaching storm that will do you some damage. This could be a domestic or business "storm."

Pigeon To dream of a flying pigeon, according to Gypsies in Yorkshire, is to expect news in the form of a letter. If you don't see the pigeon land it could be good or bad news. If you see the bird land then it is definitely good news.

Raven A favorite bird of the Gypsies. Many dream books call this a bird of ill omen but Romanis say that to dream of it signifies a family reunion, with much happiness and joy to come. If it is flying, the reunion will be unexpected; if at rest, it will be something you organize.

Swallow Flying swallows mean happiness and good fortune. Nesting swallows mean close friendship.

Vulture Represents a bitter enemy. To kill a vulture is to triumph over your enemy. To see one devouring its prey is a warning about a law suit.

BIRD'S NEST A sign of coming marriage. A nest full of eggs means success in your personal life. A nest full of baby birds presages a coming trip with friends. An empty nest means that plans for a trip will fall through. (See above concerning some individual birds' nests.)

BIRTHDAY PARTY See *Christmas Party*.

BISCUIT See *Eating/Drinking*.

BISHOP You will receive news of the death of a distant relative. (See also *Abbot*.)

BLACKBIRD See *Birds*.

BLACKBOARD See *Chalk*.

BLACKSMITH You will be very successful through your own hard work.

BLINDFOLD To have a blindfold placed over your eyes means you are seeking knowledge. To blindfold someone else means you have knowledge you should be giving to someone else.

BLIND PERSON See *Meeting*.

BLOOD The Gypsies say that to dream of blood on your hands means you will get an inheritance. To see a pool of blood means there is the opportunity for an investment that could pay off very well.

BLOSSOM To see trees in blossom indicates that you will have good luck in the future. The work you do now will be well rewarded, though you may have to wait a while to see the results. One old Gypsy woman insisted that the only meaning for dreaming of blossoms (specifically fruit tree blossoms) was a coming wedding.

BLOW To receive a blow, to be hit, by a stranger is to learn a valuable lesson. If you are hit by someone you know, then you will be rendered some service.

BLUE See *Colors*.

BOAR Beware of business associates. If you dream of being chased by a boar, you will encounter a bitter enemy. To go on a boar hunt is to labor uselessly. To kill a boar is to gain a victory over your enemies.

BOAT/SHIP To dream of a sailboat is to be complacent. However, if it is in stormy seas you are going to find yourself extremely busy. A sailboat is also a means of transport and, as such, should be considered a symbol of spiritual progression; a light, almost dilettante form. A steamship is a slow but steady method of transportation. A lifeboat is not transportation *per se* and may be considered in the Gypsies' sense, as symbolizing a need to escape; trying to get out of a difficult situation.

BOILED MEAT See *Eating/Drinking*.

BONES See *Skeleton*.

BOOKS See *Library*.

BOOTS & SHOES

BOOTS/SHOES New boots or shoes mean you will have good luck in business, possibly connected with a trip out of town. Old, worn boots or shoes indicate worries, and can mean separation from loved ones.

BOSOM A well-developed, shapely bosom or breast indicates that you can look forward to wealth and comfort. If the breasts are old and withered then you will experience sadness and, possibly, illness.

BOTTLE To dream of a full bottle is symbolic of having plenty and being willing to share with others. To see an empty bottle symbolizes a need; a yearning.

BOUQUET A sign of love. To have a bouquet presented to you is to have love offered to you. If you are the one presenting the bouquet, then you will be meeting someone who attracts you very much. To carry a bouquet means an approaching marriage. To catch a bouquet thrown at you means you will meet your true love. To throw a bouquet indicates displeasure. Faded flowers in a bouquet mean there will be sickness.

BOW See *Shooting*.

BOX To dream of a box, or boxes, full of items

indicates that you will be taking a journey. To dream of empty boxes means you will lose something which, although you seldom used it, was important to you.

BOY Gypsies say that to dream of a young boy is a sure sign of pleasures to come, both in business and in home life. If the boy is older—in his early teens—then it is a sign that hard work will bring great reward.

BRACELET A bracelet around the wrist means you will inherit a legacy. Worn higher up the arm, you will receive a gift. An ankle bracelet means you will frivolously spend an inheritance. To lose a bracelet is to let an opportunity slip through your fingers.

BRANDY Indicative of living "high off the hog" with little thought for tomorrow and little regard for your friends.

BREAD To smell bread means you will be given an opportunity to make some money. A loaf of bread handed to you could mean a new child on the way. To slice bread is to divide up your luck into small amounts. To eat fresh bread is to enjoy good friendship. To eat stale bread is to open yourself up to possible sickness.

BREAST See *Bosom*.

BRIDE To dream of a bride indicates wealth to come. A young girl dreaming of a bride will find her true love. To kiss a bride is to be assured of an increase in wealth.

BRIDGE To cross a bridge means you will overcome your difficulties. If the bridge is old, you will overcome them but it will take much work on your part. If the bridge is new and strong, you will have an easy time of it.

BRIDLE A bridle on a horse means that you are being manipulated.

BRIGAND See *Meeting*.

BROOK/STREAM Social advancement. If it is rough water, there is the possibility of social gaffes and gossip.

BROOM If you are sweeping with a broom you need to change your habits; possibly change your friends (certainly examine them and determine whether or not they are good for you). To see a broom standing in a corner means that you must examine your way of life to see if you are living up to your full potential.

BROWN See *Colors*.

BUCKET To dream of a bucket full of water, or other liquid, means that you will receive something to your advantage. If the bucket is empty you will be given an opportunity to gain something.

BULL The Romani belief is that to dream of a bull means you are going to experience financial gain. If it is a white bull, then it will be a gain in love and friendship. To be chased by a bull means you should be careful in your business dealings. To fight a bull, or be at a bullfight, means there are many different forces at work and you need to concentrate your efforts on one particular path of advancement.

BUM See *Hobo*.

BURGLARS Precarious money matters. Check into your investments and be sure they are sound.

BURIAL/FUNERAL The end of an episode in your life. Time for a new beginning. Start looking about you and consider the path you want to take.

BURN To burn any object symbolizes ridding yourself of something that is unwanted. To burn yourself is to chastise yourself for something you know you have done wrong.

BUST See *Bosom*.

BUTCHER Seeing/watching a butcher cut up meat means you must be careful not to cause gossip about your actions. To see a butcher slaughter an animal presages the death of a relative.

BUTTER See *Eating / Drinking*.

BUTTERFLY Your lover is popular and a flirt, but nothing more. In other words, he/she may flirt but always remains faithful to you.

CAB/TAXI To ride in a cab is to have good fortune. Some Romanis say it indicates a short but pleasant vacation that is coming.

CABBAGE To dream of eating cabbage means you will receive good luck. To dream of cooking cabbage means you will go into debt.

CAGE You have things well under control. If you are in the cage you will be visited by relatives for whom you do not care.

CAKE Eating cake means good luck. Strangely, if a woman dreams she is eating wedding cake it means she will have a period of bad luck. To bake a cake means you will bring your own luck.

CALF Seeing a calf at a cow's udder in your dream is a sign that you will achieve your ambitions. If a young woman dreams of seeing a calf it means her husband will be a good provider.

CAMEL Good things coming into your life. If you dream of a whole caravan of camels then it will be money that is coming.

CAMEO BROOCH You will achieve a position of importance with people working under you.

CAMPGROUND The Romani *Atching tan* symbolizes a grand reunion to come, with much celebration and enjoyment. You will be getting together with people you haven't seen for a long time—friends and relatives—and exchanging news and gossip.

CANAL To dream of a boat on a canal signifies that your love life will become complicated. If a horse pulls the boat then, however complicated it becomes, it will eventually even out and flow smoothly again.

CANARY See *Birds*.

CANDLE An unlit candle is a symbol of opportunity. A lit candle symbolizes revelation; that which was hidden will be revealed to you. To dream of a candelabra or chandelier is a sign of taking on new responsibility.

CANNON A firing cannon means achievement; accomplishment. A stationary cannon, with the cannonballs piled beside it, means opportunity.

CANOE Success in love. If you are in a canoe that tips over you will have a quarrel with your lover.

CAPE To be wearing a cape means you are trying to cover up some action of which you are ashamed.

CAPON See *Eating / Drinking*.

CAPTAIN To be captain of a ship is to be in command, so to dream of being a captain means that you will have major decision(s) to make which could affect many people. To meet with a ship's captain means that you will be able to influence whomever is in the position to make a decision.

CAR See *Automobile*.

CARAVAN See *Camel*.

CARDINAL See *Abbot*. Also see *Meeting*.

CARDS, PLAYING Symbolize life, according to Romanis. If you dream you are winning when playing cards, you will do well and profit in life. If you are losing, you will suffer some setbacks. If you are shuffling cards, there will be decisions to make. If cards are dealt to you, you will find yourself with a sudden problem to solve.

CAROUSEL You will have many opportunities, any one of which could be advantageous. Choose one and stick with it; don't keep changing your mind.

CARPET/RUG A rich, ornamental/oriental carpet means you will receive riches. An old and worn carpet means you will fall on hard times.

CARRIAGE/WAGGON/VARDO The *vardo* is the Gypsies' house-on-wheels. If you dream of a vardo or waggon approaching you, there are people coming to visit you, or bringing news to you (which could be good or bad). If the waggon is going away, you will be parted from a loved one. A stationary or passing waggon means things will stabilize and not change for some time. If you are riding in the waggon, you are making progress (and again consider the spiritual connotations, with this being a means of transportation). If you are driving the waggon yourself, you are in charge of your own life and able to make decisions.

CASTANETS You will suffer many minor irritations.

CASTLE Ambition. You have high ideals and a great desire to advance yourself. Some Gypsies say that to dream of castles can also mean a coming journey that will take you where you have never been before. It could lead to adventure, opportunity, mystery. Be ready for anything!

CAT A sleeping cat means that someone is plotting against you. A cat washing itself means you need to get your affairs in order. A cat walking or running is a sign of missed opportunity. If a cat scratches you, you will be involved in a law suit. To hear a cat's meow is to be warned of impending unpleasantness.

CATERPILLAR Beware of false friends.

CAVALRY An opportunity to make a great deal of money, if you are very careful. If the cavalry is charging, you will get a promotion in your work.

CAVE/CAVERN To see a cave or cavern means there will be an opportunity to go back and correct something you have done wrong. To be inside a cavern is to have security, if only for a short while.

CELLAR If you open the door to a cellar you will uncover a lot of unsavory gossip. If you find yourself down in a cellar, you are mixing with undesirable company.

CEMETERY A well kept cemetery, with flowers on the graves, indicates that you will have many friends who will be faithful to you for many years. An unkempt cemetery indicates loss of friends; acquaintances rather than close friends.

CHAIN A restriction. To be bound in chains

is to be held back from doing what you want to do. (See also *Dress*.)

CHALK A stick of chalk, or any chalk writing on a blackboard, indicates temporary advantage that could easily slip away. If it is writing, take note of what is written.

CHALLENGE If you are challenged by another, you will be involved in an argument with the opposite sex. If you are the one who issues the challenge, you will argue with someone of your own sex.

CHAMPAGNE Symbolizes money. A bottle of champagne is the chance to make money. To drink champagne is to receive money. To toast a newly married couple with champagne is to be assured of success in business.

CHANDELIER See *Candle*.

CHECKERS Playing checkers indicates you will be involved in an argument. (See also *Chess*.)

CHEESE See *Eating/Drinking*.

CHERRIES See *Fruits*.

CHESS Playing chess indicates you will be

involved in an argument with family members. (See also *Checkers*.)

CHESTNUT / CHESTNUT TREE Dreaming of a chestnut means you will be healthy and strong. A chestnut tree indicates you will have sons.

CHICKEN See *Hen*.

CHILD See *Baby*. See also *Bread* and *Meeting*.

CHIMES See *Bells*.

CHIMNEY The Gypsies say that dreaming of a chimney that is not smoking means you are in need of a sexual outlet. A smoking chimney means you are involved in an affair.

CHINA See *Earthenware*.

CHOCOLATE Eating or drinking chocolate means that you will soon be going through an illness, though not a serious one.

CHOIR To dream that you are singing in a choir means that you will do something for others that will earn you great respect.

CHRISTMAS / BIRTHDAY PARTY To be

at a party means that you will be meeting with your lover the following day, and will have a wonderful time.

CHRISTMAS TREE You will have a large family.

CHURCH You are going to receive some bad news. If you are inside the church, you are going to become very depressed and very pessimistic.

CHURCHYARD The Gypsies assert that dreaming of a churchyard means you will soon find yourself in a lawyer's office.

CIGARETTE See *Smoke*.

CIRCUS To dream of a circus means you are going to be so active, in both your social and business life, that you won't have time to do many of the things you would really like to do.

CLOCK Seeing a clock on a building signifies that you will receive some recognition. A small clock indicates that you have to reach a quick decision. To wind a clock means you have much work to do to get a reasonable return. To hear a clock chiming is a warning that time is running out. If possible try to remember the time shown on a clock in your dreams or the number of times it strikes— this could be significant. (See *Numbers*. See also *Alarm Clock*.)

COBWEB A sign of laziness, unless there is also a spider present. (See also *Spider*.)

COCK Pride, success, power. Fighting cocks mean there will be a challenge to your position.

COFFEE To drink or smell coffee is a sign of long life.

COFFIN Generally a good sign. The Gypsies say that to see someone lying in a coffin means that you will live to see your children grown and married. To see yourself in a coffin means you will enjoy excellent health throughout your life. But, to see someone famous in a coffin means the possibility of war.

COLONEL/MILITARY OFFICER For a woman to dream of a military officer means she will have many boyfriends. For a man the dream means that he will achieve recognition in later life.

COLORS:

Blue Gypsies associate the color blue with the sky; dark blue with the night sky. They say that to have that color especially prominent in a dream indicates a desire to get out into the open, to get away. Perhaps a need for a vacation.

Brown The color of the earth. A need to get down to your roots, or to the basics of your problems.

Green The color of the grass. When green is prominent in your dreams it indicates growth and abundance.

Orange The color for life and new beginnings (perhaps tied in with the sunrise).

Purple A color of richness and luxury.

Red The universal color for danger and excitement.

Yellow Many Gypsy vardos are painted yellow. It is a color for happiness, and for love and family togetherness.

COMET To see a comet rush across the sky in your dreams means you will be having unexpected good fortune.

COMPASS To dream of a compass means you are uncertain as to which direction you should proceed.

CONCERT If you attend, or perform at, a concert, you will be able to play a musical instrument. If the music in the dream is terrible and off-key then you will have arguments with relatives.

CONFETTI You will have an exciting experience with someone who seems very glamorous to you.

CONVENT There will be restrictions imposed upon you.

COOKIE See *Eating/Drinking*.

CORKSCREW You have a very inquisitive friend who could cause you harm.

CORN Corn on the cob indicates coming financial gain. Corn growing in a field means you will have a good and happy marriage. Popcorn means a sudden, unexpected windfall.

CORONATION You will earn a lot more money but the increased wealth will bring with it far greater responsibility.

CORPSE A "reverse symbol." If you are the corpse you will be assured of a long, happy and healthy life. If someone you don't know is the corpse, you will have a long and interesting life (not necessarily happy nor healthy).

COTTAGE/HOUSE To dream of a cottage or house means that you will live a sedate life; quite happy but with no great excitement in it.

COW A sign of home and comfort. You will want for little. If you are milking the cow then you will have to work hard most of your life but will be well rewarded for it.

CRAB Signifies the possibility of a lawsuit,

involving someone you thought of as a friend.

CRADLE If there is a child in the cradle then you will have a child. If the cradle is empty it means you will be relocating.

CREAM If you are drinking the cream you will receive an unexpected gift. If you spill cream you will have to pay an unexpected bill.

CRICKET To dream of seeing a cricket, or hearing a cricket chirruping, foretells long life and happy times ahead.

CROCODILE/ALLIGATOR You will have an accident, brought about by trying to avoid your enemies.

CROQUET Playing croquet means you will have a very pleasant time with close friends.

CROSS An equal-armed cross is a sign of good luck to come. If the cross is enclosed in a circle it means there will be financial good luck.

CROSSROADS You will have a decision to make that could affect the rest of your life.

CROW See *Birds*.

CROWN A warning. Be very careful in all decisions you make, especially business decisions. If it is a paper crown (as at a party) you are riding for a fall.

CRUCIFIX You will experience shame and humiliation.

CURLS If you dream you have curly hair, you will be much sought after on the social scene, and much admired by the opposite sex. If it is someone else who has the curls, beware of criticizing others, especially the opposite sex.

If curls are cut off, you will suddenly find yourself without friends.

DAFFODILS Sign of an early marriage.

DAGGER If you are holding the dagger you are going to antagonize someone. If you are not actually holding the dagger, it will be someone you do not wish to harm. (See also *Knife*.)

DAISIES White daisies indicate a faithful spouse. Yellow daisies show a spouse's jealousy due to your receiving too much attention from someone else.

DANCING See *Ballroom*.

DANDELIONS Represent false friends. If there are a lot of dandelions ... watch out!

DAUGHTER You are going to be very worried over the actions of someone else, but your worries will turn out to be needless.

DEAD See *Corpse*.

DEAF If you dream that you are deaf it means you will quickly be relieved of all your worries. If you are trying to talk to someone who is deaf, you will experience a number of minor irritations.

DEATHBED To be on your deathbed means you will soon receive a visit from someone you haven't seen in a very long time. To be at someone else's deathbed means you will be going to visit someone you haven't seen in a long time.

DEBT To dream you are in debt means you will receive money from an older relative.

DECANTERS The number of decanters indicates the number of children you will have. Full decanters indicate girls; empty or only partially full decanters indicate boys.

DECISION To ponder a problem in a dream and then reach a decision means that you will start a new project, a new job, or relocate.

DEER A female deer is a sign of hard times to come. An antlered deer means you are in for a long, hard battle. (See also *Stag*.)

DELAY When there seems to be a long delay in your dream, with you waiting for something to happen, it means that you will receive a surprise that could either be pleasant or unpleasant.

DENTIST To dream you are at the dentist means that you will have a sudden change of fortune. To have a tooth extracted means you will meet a new love.

DESERT To find yourself in a desert is a sign that you are searching for knowledge.

DESK If the desk is cluttered you need to reorganize things in your life and get a system of priorities. If the desk is bare you should look for new interests, new hobbies.

DEVIL A devil (*Beng* is the Romani word) appearing in your dreams is an indication that your friends are insincere.

DEW Romanis say that it is a very good omen to dream that you see the dew on the early morning grass. It indicates that you will be lucky in love and that your life will always be happy.

DIAMOND A single diamond is an indication of social success. A number of diamonds, as in a necklace or brooch, mean a long, happy marriage.

DICE A die, or dice, being cast is a sign of family worries to come. Throwing a lucky combination indicates short-lived happiness.

DINNER To dine alone, or with your lover, means you will be forgiving someone or receiving forgiveness from someone. To dine with a number of people denotes petty bickering and quarreling.

DITCH Deceit; trouble. Be cautious. To fall into a ditch is a warning of coming injury.

DIVING BELL/SUIT To be submerged beneath the sea in a diving bell or diving suit signifies that you will find yourself in a predicament over which you have no control but which you will nonetheless find fascinating.

DOCK See *Port*.

DOCTOR Watch your health if you dream of a doctor. (The Romani word for doctor is *mulled-mushengro* which, literally translated, means "dead man maker!") You are susceptible to colds, the flu, or worse—anything that may be going around. This is true whether you dream of meeting with a doctor or if you are the doctor yourself. (See also *Meeting*.)

DOG To play with a dog is to expect to suffer from former extravagance. To be chased by a dog is to lose a friend. A running dog means there will be loss from a lawsuit. A barking dog indicates that you will become close friends with people you had previously tended to mistrust. To be bitten by a dog means you'll have an argument with your spouse. To hear a dog barking is a warning of danger to come.

DOMINOES Beware of any form of investment presented to you.

DONKEY See *Ass*.

DOOR See *Back Door*.

DOVE See *Birds*.

DRAGON A dragon symbolizes a dangerous undertaking. If you slay a dragon you achieve great success.

DRAGONFLY You'll be taking a short trip by air.

DRAPERIES Rich and luxurious draperies reflect your life, which will be rich and luxurious. But old, torn drapes indicate great hardships to come.

DRESS, ARTICLES OF:

Chain A chain belt, or similar article of dress, denotes union.

Embroidery Love that could grow to something wonderful.

Fan Pride, touched with vanity.

Feathers White: a great sense of humor. Black: a pessimistic attitude.

Gauze Affected modesty.

Gloves Pleasure to come that will be all too brief.

Hat A new hat is the sign of a surprise. A hat that is too big is a sign of ostentation. A hat too small shows that you are overly modest.

Linen Fortune; abundance.

Muff Ostentation. You too often do things on a whim.

Necklace See *Necklace* (separate listing).

Needles Disappointment in love.

Pearls Tears.

Pins Contradiction.

Ribbons Change of employment.

Rings Approaching marriage.

Satin/Silk Financial gain.

Scissors Enemies; hatred.

Shoes See *Boots* (separate listing).

Veil You have something to hide.

DRINKING GLASS To see a number of drinking glasses means there will be sudden arguments between you and your lover. A single glass indicates the need for a short vacation. To break a glass means that you are going to have to suddenly change your plans.

DROWNING If you are drowning it means you will be shamed. If someone else is drowning you will be involved in a minor scandal.

DRUM A sign of communication. If you are beating a drum you will write an important letter. If you hear a drum being beaten you will receive an important letter.

DUCK/GOOSE A generally favorable omen. A quacking duck or honking goose is the herald of good news to come. To shoot a duck is to make a mistake; to "stick your foot in it." To see a duck or ducks flying overhead means good news is coming if they fly from left to right, and bad news if they fly from right to left.

DUEL Indicates that you are unsure of a recent decision that you made. Whether or not you win the duel will indicate whether or not you were right in that decision.

DUNGEON To be locked up in a dungeon means you are being controlled by others.

DWARF See *Meeting*.

EAGLE See *Birds*.

EARRING(S) To be wearing one earring means you will be with the one you love. To be wearing two earrings means you will be flirting with a number of people.

EARTHENWARE/CHINA Personal property will be stolen.

EARTHQUAKE You are very unsure of yourself and need to do something to gain a little self-confidence.

EASY CHAIR You have been working too hard and deserve a vacation.

EATING/DRINKING:

> **Boiled/Roast Meat** You will tend to be melancholy and dwell a lot on the past.

> **Bread** See *Baker/Bakery* and *Bread* (separate listings).

> **Butter** You will have good fortune mixed with sadness. Wealth to come, but at a price.

> **Cake** See *Cake* (separate listing).

> **Capon** You have been deceived in your affections.

Cheese Vexation; frustration, but final success.

Cookie (Biscuit) There will be great rejoicing.

Eels Malicious enemies.

Eggs A wealth of family love.

Ham You will meet a very jolly person.

Honey You are being falsely sweet to someone . . . and it shows!

Macaroni A symbol of great distress.

Millet A sign of poverty.

Mustard There will be a number of family quarrels.

Oysters To dream that you are eating oysters is a very favorable sign, usually signifying a large family. If you are married, your spouse will be very much in love with you and you will have several children. If you are not married, you soon will be and then will go on to have children.

Pastry To be eating pastries means you will miss an important appointment. You could suffer illness at a most inconvenient time.

Rice As with millet, a sign of poverty.

Salad Various embarrassments.

Salt You will be recognized for great wisdom.

Sausages You will be accused of interfering in someone else's love affair.

Soup You will return to good health.

Vinegar You will labor in vain for a while.

ECHO To hear your voice echoing means that you are being mocked behind your back.

ECLIPSE Of the sun denotes coming loss. Of the moon means profit.

EELS See *Eating/Drinking*.

EGGS See *Eating/Drinking*.

ELEPHANT A symbol of power. To ride one,

you have the power. To see one pass by, you will be in touch with power and may be able to make use of it.

EMBRACE/HUG If it is an affectionate one it denotes a happy home life. If it is a passionate one, you should beware of your feelings getting out of hand.

EMBROIDERY See *Dress*.

ENGINE To dream of a railroad locomotive, or steam engine, means that you have the ability to do anything you wish. You can succeed at anything to which you put your mind. (See also *Train*.)

ENVELOPE To address an envelope means you will soon meet with that person. If you receive an envelope, you will have an opportunity. If you mail an envelope you will do someone a favor which they will appreciate and later repay. (See also *Letters*.)

EPITAPH You will make an indiscretion.

ERRAND If you send someone else on an errand, you are fearful that your spouse is being unfaithful. If you are sent on an errand, you are planning on being unfaithful.

EXECUTION To witness an execution means that you are thinking of divorcing your spouse, or leaving your lover. To be the one about to be executed means you are feeling guilty about infidelities.

EXPLOSIONS If you dream of explosions connected with quarrying, tunneling, etc., you have a lazy streak and would rather avoid work. If you dream of explosions that destroy buildings and people, you are afraid of firm commitments, especially where love is concerned.

EYEPATCH Shows an interest in the occult; things secret.

FALCON See *Birds*.

FALLING Falling dreams are not uncommon. The Gypsies say they indicate that you are unhappy, especially with personal relationships, and want to get out of a situation.

FALSE TEETH To see false teeth, or someone noticeably wearing false teeth, means that someone is putting up a false front in dealing with you. Check your business contacts carefully. If you dream that you are wearing false teeth, it means that you are not being totally honest in what you say.

FAME To dream of being famous means that you have high expectations but are in for big disappointments.

FAMINE A sign of guilt about your spending. You unconsciously feel that while you are being extravagant, others are starving.

FAN See *Dress*.

FARM/FARMER As a result of your hard work you will reap a fine reward. However, if you dream of a farm that is run-down it forebodes financial losses.

FAT/FATNESS To dream that you are fat is an unconscious acknowledgment that you are overeating.

FAUCET A dripping faucet means you are wasting money, in small amounts but consistently. A running faucet means you are throwing away a great deal of money. A faucet that is turned off means you must exercise caution, for there is a possibility that you will be tempted to spend more money than you can afford.

FAWN You will shortly meet with a wonderful person whom you will desire very much.

FEAST Tremendous success financially. You will receive far more than you ever expected. (See also *Eating/Drinking*.)

FEATHER A white feather means good luck coming your way. A black feather means financial loss. To see a number of feathers floating in the air, whatever their color, means you will have a chance to fulfill your desires. (See also *Dress*.)

FEATHER BED Easy times ahead.

FENCE To dream of a fence means you feel restricted. To climb over a fence means you are desperate to get out of a particular situation.

FERRY A ferryboat shows that you will have the opportunity to bring two divided parties together.

FIELDS If the fields are overgrown and wild, you will lose control of things unless you get down to a lot of hard work. If the fields are plowed you will have a wonderful opportunity to "plant seeds." If the fields are rich with harvest, you will receive abundance.

FIGS See *Fruits*.

FINGER To dream of a finger pointing at you means that you have done something underhanded and are afraid of being found out.

FIRE A low, smoldering fire shows that you are repressing some strong desire. A blazing fire means that things are getting out of hand. If you set a fire, you are planning to do something that could have a tremendous impact on your life. To put out a fire means that you will win over people who have been opposing you. If you are sitting by a campfire, you will find comfort and happiness.

FISH To see a fish swimming indicates joy and success. To catch a fish means that there will be illness in the family. To eat a fish means you will fall sick.

FLAG To dream you see a flag waving means you may be in great danger from enemies. To carry a flag, or raise a flag, means you will receive some mark of distinction.

FLAME See *Fire*.

FLATTERY If someone unduly flatters you in your dreams the Gypsies say it means that you are feeling very good about yourself, but beware of becoming egotistical.

FLEAS Small irritations. Small problems in your business and private affairs.

FLIES Someone is jealous because of your success. To swat at flies in your dream is to irritate that person and flaunt your success.

FLIRT If you are the one flirting, you are not happy in your present situation. If someone is flirting with you, you can expect a mild love affair to develop.

FLOUR To see flour, either packaged or at the mill, means it is a good time to invest, but don't put all your money into one venture.

FLOWERS/GARLAND A symbol for hope, especially where love is concerned. (See also individual flower names.)

FLUTE The sound of a flute shows a happy home life. To play the flute shows love for your family.

FLYING To dream that you are flying through the air (and most common is to dream that you are using a swimming motion to do this) indicates that you feel restricted. You want to be free to carry out your desires. The Gypsies say this is often tied in with sexual frustration. To dream of flying in an airplane is slightly different, indicating that you want to hurry things along; you are anxious to get somewhere much faster than you are going.

FOG/FOGHORN Uncertainty. To dream that you are in a thick mist or fog means that your way in life will often seem dark and perplexing. But, by perseverance and by applying yourself to your own self development, you will come out of the dark into the light. To be completely lost in a fog means you are frustrated, not knowing what decision to make. To hear a foghorn means that there are troubled times ahead.

FOOD See *Eating/Drinking*.

FOOTMAN See *Meeting*.

FOREST To be in a large, beautiful forest means you will find peace and tranquility. If you are lost in a forest, then you will have family quarrels.

FORTUNETELLING (*Dukkering*) To dream of having your fortune told indicates that you will have a sudden change of fortune, that might be for the better or might be worse. If you are the fortuneteller, it means that you will be having flashes of insight into the future. Pay particular attention to any "hunches" you have in the next few days.

FOUNTAIN A spouting fountain symbolizes a happy marriage. A small fountain is a sign of love that is capable of developing into something wonderful. A fountain that dries up means that you are heading for the rocks, where love is concerned.

FOX Cleverness; cunning. If you see a fox passing by, you will be the clever one. If you are on a fox hunt, beware of others. A vixen with her cubs indicates a clever woman.

FROG You will progress "by leaps and bounds," say the Gypsies. If you see a frog sitting still, it is not yet definite that you will be moving forward in the near future. But if you see it jumping . . . hold on!

FRUITS:

Apples Green apples indicate fickle friendships. Ripe red apples show true friendship you can depend upon. Baked apples, or apples in a pie, mean great expectations followed by disappointment.

Apricots Good health and contentment.

Cherries Black cherries: deception by your lover. Red cherries: you can have complete trust in your lover.

Figs If you see figs growing on a tree, you will encounter a foreigner who could be very good for you and/or your business. If you are eating figs, you will gain new knowledge.

Grapes Rejoicing; celebration. To eat grapes: satisfaction with yourself and your work.

Lemons Symbolize struggle. Lemons frequently indicate that you will marry someone of a sour disposition. If you dream of actually squeezing lemons, then you will have a hard struggle to make ends meet. To suck a lemon indicates a possible legal suit against you. To drink lemon juice is to be drawn into a court case.

Melons Any sort of melon indicates a

coming journey across water.

Nuts Conjugal happiness. Eating nuts, of any type, means that you will gratify your sexual desires. To break open a nut means you will have a job getting what you want but, when you do get it, it will be well worth it.

Olives Much like nuts, a sexual symbol. Black olives indicate you will enjoy sexual favors with someone you already know and will spend time with close friends. Green olives indicate you will enjoy sexual favors with someone you do not know yet, and will make new friends.

Oranges Signify amusement. To eat oranges means you will be well entertained.

Peaches Presage a journey over land.

Pears You will unexpectedly be invited to a party.

Plums Unchanging friendship. Someone who's loyalty you were wondering about will prove to be true.

Pomegranate A symbol of sexual power. To dream of eating pomegranates means you will sexually dominate the opposite sex.

Strawberries This fruit means unexpected good fortune, both in the home and in business.

FUNERAL News of the death of someone not close to you. The death will indirectly benefit you. An unexpected inheritance. (See also *Burial*.)

GAG To dream that your mouth is gagged, or stopped in some way, means that you will be kissed in the near future.

GAMBLING You are not satisfied with the direction your life is taking. You want to make changes just for the sake of changing, even if they are reckless changes. (See also Chapter 7, "Dreaming for Profit.")

GARLAND See *Flowers*.

GARLIC Symbolizes prosperity.

GARTER A symbol of rank and recognition. You will be promoted but this will place you in a more vulnerable position. You will have to be much more careful in considering the consequences of your words and actions.

GAS To dream that you smell gas means that you have false friends. To see a high, bright gas flame means you will have a love affair with a rich person. If the flame is low, the affair will be with a person who will involve you in scandal.

GATE To find your way blocked by a closed gate means you will be frustrated in your desires. If the gate is open, and you can pass through, then your plans will go fairly smoothly with only minor hitches.

GAUZE See *Dress*.

GHOST To see a ghost means a distant relative is displeased with you. To see the ghost of someone you know often presages the death of that person (though not always).

GIANT To dream of a giant means that you

feel insecure and have an inferiority complex.

GIFT A gift received from a man in a dream means the possibility of danger. Received from a woman, it is a sign of spite. If you give the gift, you will be relieving yourself of problems and worries.

GLOVES See *Dress*.

GOAT To dream of goats is a sign of prosperity. But if you get butted by a goat, you will suffer a loss. To be milking a goat means several small setbacks but final triumph.

GOGGLES You will discover something to your advantage; something which your enemy hoped you would overlook.

GOLD To dream of gold, say the Gypsies, means you have a tendency to be greedy. If, in your dream, you buy gold you will lose friends because of this greed. But if you are mining gold, you will overcome the tendency.

GOLDFISH You will break with your present lover, which will cause much heartache. But as a result of this you will meet someone far superior, who will bring you great joy, love and happiness.

GOLD WATCH You will receive some public recognition.

GOLF You will live a long life and will have the opportunity to correct many mistakes that you have made.

GOOSE See *Duck*.

GRANDMOTHER To dream of a grand-mother, or *puri dai* as the Gypsies call her, means that you are in need of help and advice. The grandmother is the "old wise one" of the family. She is always consulted when big decisions are to be made which affect the whole tribe. If, in your dream, she gives you advice...follow it! She will not be wrong.

GRANDPARENT See *Meeting*.

GRAPES See *Fruits*.

GRASS Deep, green grass is a sure sign of a coming marriage. Poor, worn grass is a sign of hardship to come.

GRASSHOPPER A bad sign, usually signifying financial losses to come.

GRAVE/GRAVESTONES See *Cemetery*.

GREEN See *Colors*.

GUITAR To hear the music of a guitar, or to

watch a guitarist, means you will be made happy by the one you love. If you are the person playing the guitar, beware of swindlers.

GUN Guns are generally tied in with arguments and disagreements; small guns (such as handguns) signify small arguments; large guns, big arguments. If you hear a gunshot, an argument involving you will soon develop. If you shoot a gun, you will be the cause of the argument. If someone shoots a gun at you (regardless of whether they hit you or miss), it means you will be badly hurt by a coming argument.

GUNPOWDER There is a plot developing to overthrow you; to cast you out of an important position. The plotters are people you had thought to be your friends. (See also *Powder Flask*.)

GYPSY To dream of a Gypsy, or Gypsies, is a sure sign that you will be wandering/traveling in the near future. If you dream that you are a Gypsy, you will enjoy a wonderfully happy marriage. If you are with a group of Gypsies, you are going to a reunion. If you dream of a Gypsy telling your fortune (*dukkering*), listen to what he or she says; it is important.

HAIL Symbolizes trouble and distress.

HAIR To dream of short hair means unhappiness. Long hair is a sign of good fortune. If your hair is disheveled and unkempt, there are annoyances and arguments coming, while well-groomed hair shows abundance. To cut your hair, or see someone have theirs cut, means you are working against yourself; hurting yourself by your actions.

HAM See *Eating/Drinking*.

HAMMER Using a hammer indicates that you are being very determined and forceful . . . perhaps a little too forceful.

HAMMOCK If you are lying in a hammock by yourself it is a sign of selfishness. To be lying in one with someone of the opposite sex means you will be attending a social function.

HANDCUFFS Your hands are tied. There is something you really want to do but you are being prevented from doing it.

HANDKERCHIEF If your lover gives you a handkerchief it is a sign of faithfulness. To pick up a handkerchief that has been dropped is to pick up someone else's troubles. To blow your nose with a handkerchief means there will be news of sickness in the family.

HANGMAN See *Meeting*.

HARE/RABBIT To see a hare or rabbit sitting still means you will have the chance to increase your prosperity. A whole warren of rabbits means much increase in your fortunes. A black rabbit signifies a high risk situation with your finances. A white rabbit is a sign of a legacy.

HARNESS A horse in a harness is a sign that someone has dominance and regulation over you, yet has your own betterment at heart. If you are harnessing a horse then you are the one who is going to dominate.

HAT See *Dress*.

HATCHET See *Axe*.

HAWK See *Birds*.

HAY The possibility of an inheritance. To be mowing hay signifies that it will be money that you have earned.

HEADSCARF See *Bandanna*.

HEARSE To see a hearse go by means that you will be starting a new job. To be riding in, or driving, a hearse means you will be relocating.

HEDGEHOG See *Porcupine*.

HEDGES The Gypsies say that to dream of

hedges means you will be involved in some important discussions. The Romani word for a conference is *bouri-pennen* which literally translates as "hedge gathering," from the fact that such a meeting often takes place along, or under, the hedgerow.

HEN/CHICKEN Profit; considerable gain. A hen with chicks means you will be granted a favor you have been seeking. A hen laying an egg is good fortune. To hear a clucking hen means consolation for some hurt. To feed chickens means you will suffer some minor annoyances.

HERMIT See *Meeting*.

HILL If you climb up a hill you will succeed in your undertakings. If you stand and look at a hill, you will be met with a challenge. To stand on a hill top means you will be in a secure, comfortable position.

HOBO You have set down your roots and will be staying where you presently live for a very long time.

HOE You will enjoy good health and spirits for a long time to come, though some Gypsies claim it means profit from selling and trading.

HOLE To see a hole means the possibility of an accident. However, to fall into a hole means your lover is very sweet and loving!

HOLLY A person of the opposite sex will charm and captivate you, but you should beware for they have ulterior motives.

HONEY See *Eating/Drinking*.

HONEYMOON To dream you are on your honeymoon means there is going to be a "rude awakening" coming to you in the very near future. Be prepared for not-so-pleasant surprises.

HOOD To dream of wearing a hood means you have something to hide.

HORSE Good fortune, in business and in the home. A white, or gray, horse indicates prosperity. A black, or brown, one indicates power and position. To be mounting a horse, indicates you will be well rewarded for work done. To shoe a horse is to be assured of comfort in your old age. A stallion represents sexual power. A mare is sexual fulfillment.

HORSEMAN See *Meeting*.

HOUNDS To dream of hounds in full cry

means that you will have plenty on your table for the coming year.

HOUSE See *Cottage*.

HUG See *Embrace*.

HUNGER Temporary poverty.

HURDY-GURDY See *Organ Grinder*.

ICE Symbolizes a betrayed confidence. Secrets you have shared have not remained secret. (See *Icicles*.)

ICICLES To dream that you see a number of long, bright icicles hanging down means that bright and beautiful prospects will be yours in the future. If you are single, you will marry someone who will make you very happy.

INCENSE To burn or smell incense means that you will be taking an interest in New Age, metaphysical material.

INK To be writing, using a pen and ink, means you will betray a confidence. To spill ink means you will be exposed.

INSECTS To be bothered by small insects means that you are restless and need to change jobs or to relocate.

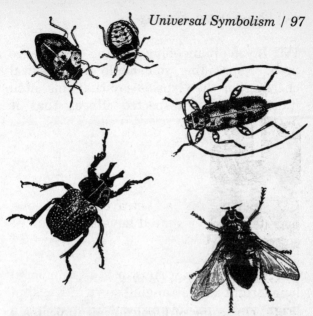

INTERRACIAL MARRIAGE A sign that a stranger from a far distance will be visiting you and will greatly influence your life.

INTOXICATION To dream that you are drunk means that you should guard against reckless spending. To dream of meeting a drunk means you should beware of financial losses.

ISLAND To see an island means that those you think are your friends are not really that close or caring. If you dream of being alone on an island it is a sign of loneliness and frustration.

IVY If you dream of ivy growing over a large area, or spreading, you should get a medical checkup for the Gypsies say that this often indicates an unsuspected illness that is developing.

JACKASS See *Ass/Donkey*.

JAIL Dreaming of being in jail indicates a feeling of guilt for something you have done that was wrong but that you hoped to get away with.

JAM/JELLY To dream of putting up jam preserves means you will develop good friends among your neighbors.

JESTER To dream of watching a court jester means that you are embarrassed about something a close friend or relative has done. If you are the jester, you are embarrassed about something you have done.

JEWELED RING A cheap, flashy ring

means you will have a minor ailment. A tasteful, expensive ring means you will be robust with excellent health.

JIG To dream of dancing a jig is a sign that someone is in love with you. If you watch someone else dancing a jig, you will fall in love.

JILTED To be jilted in your dreams means your lover is unfaithful to you. If you jilt someone, then you are planning on being unfaithful to your lover.

JOCKEY Dreaming of a jockey in a horse race means that you feel you have many ideas but too little time in which to work at them.

JUDGE See *Meeting*.

JUGGLER You are of a very competitive nature.

KETTLE (a Gypsy *kavvi*) A bright copper kettle signifies great domestic comfort. You will enjoy a very happy home life. If the kettle is black, cast-iron, you will have many children and be very close to them. If the kettle is boiling, and spouting steam, you will receive good news from a relative.

KEYS You are a practical and sensible person. To fit a key into a lock shows that you are very capable and adaptable.

KISS According to the Gypsies this is another "opposite": if you dream you are kissing your lover you are due for a quarrel. To be kissing someone you don't know means you will get into a fight. To kiss a child means you will be made to look foolish.

KITCHEN A friend is coming to visit unexpectedly.

KITE To dream of flying a kite means that you feel you are not up to your job.

KNAPSACK A need to get away and be by yourself for a while. You need a vacation and/or a change of scene.

KNEES To see or admire someone's knees means you will meet an attractive stranger. To be down on your knees means you will shortly have to ask someone's forgiveness.

KNIFE A sign of quarrels. A knife worn in the belt signifies a broken love affair. A closed jackknife, or pocketknife, means the quarrel will not be serious and will soon be patched up. (See also *Dagger*.)

KNITTING NEEDLES Your lover will be very industrious in making your marriage a happy one. If you are the one knitting in the dream, then it is you on whom the bulk of the responsibility will fall to make the marriage a success.

KNOT(S) If you dream of tying knots in a rope you are making problems for yourself.

LABORER See *Meeting*.

LACE CURTAINS Frivolity. You may have a light *affaire*, or you may indulge in a little gambling.

LADDER You aspire to greater things; climbing a ladder shows you will achieve them. If you climb a ladder to enter a house through a window, you would not be averse to doing something illegal to get ahead! If you fall from a ladder you may run afoul of the law.

LADY See *Meeting*.

LAMB To see lambs in a field means you will find inner peace and happiness.

LAME PERSON See *Meeting*.

LAMP/LANTERN To see a lantern indicates that you will achieve a breakthrough in something which has been frustrating you. To light a lantern (or switch on a light) means you will be acting in a joint venture with a friend. To extinguish a lantern means you will break up a partnership.

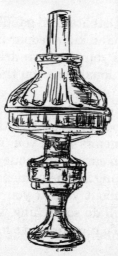

LARK See *Birds*.

LAWYER See *Meeting*.

LEATHER Indicates a good, steady position; something you can rely on.

LEAVES If the leaves are green and healthy, your love life will blossom. If the leaves are brown and falling, your love life will be in the doldrums.

LEECH You will have to face up to family obligations that you have been trying to avoid.

LEMON See *Fruits*.

LEOPARD Ostentation; gaudiness; pretension. To hunt and kill a leopard indicates you should assess your taste in dress—you may not be as fashionable as you think!

LETTERS You will make a discovery that will benefit you. To receive a letter containing good news means that you will have the opportunity to earn more money. To receive a letter containing bad news means that people are talking about you. If you are writing a letter, you will do something which you will later regret. To receive a love letter indicates that you will be meeting someone who will interest you very much. If you are writing a love letter, you will soon have a short, but very enjoyable, love affair.

LETTUCE To dream of lettuce is good, according to the Gypsies. For a woman it signifies a wonderful time to come with her lover(s). For a man it signifies the attention of a number of beautiful women.

LIBRARY/BOOKS If you see a whole library of books it means you will be greatly appreciated by people with whom you do business. To read a book in your dreams means that secrets will be revealed to you. To be given a book similarly means that you will be told a secret.

LIFEBOAT To be rescued by a lifeboat means you will gain a position of importance in your community.

LIGHTHOUSE You will be awarded a medal or given some recognition for services you have done.

LIGHTNING Trouble brought about by a woman you have been close to (though not a relative). To see lightning strike a tree or a building means you will be involved in a court case brought by this woman. (See also *Rain* and *Thunder and Lightning*.)

LILIES Joy; pleasure; great success in love.

LINEN See *Dress*.

LION You have great dignity and are much admired by others. A captive lion means lasting friendship. To be surprised by a lion indicates treachery on the part of a friend. To hear a lion roaring is a sign of opportunity to come.

LIQUOR/LIQUEURS You may do something you will very much regret afterwards.

LIZARD You need to watch your health and your diet in particular. You have an unhealthy body.

LOAF See *Baker/Bakery* and *Bread*.

LOCK You are getting into something that is forbidden. Be very careful.

LOCKET Signifies a long-term, affectionate relationship that will bring you great joy and happiness.

LOCKSMITH See *Meeting*.

LOCOMOTIVE See *Engine*.

LOLLIPOP You will receive an unexpected gift from an admirer of the opposite sex.

LOOKING-GLASS See *Mirror*.

LORD See *Meeting*.

LOTTERY TICKET You could be a winner! If you can see (and remember) the number, bet on it. If you are given a lottery ticket in your dream, you will become very successful.

LOVE LETTER See *Letter*.

LOVEMAKING If you watch others making love your plans will be successful. If you are making love yourself, you will receive great satisfaction from what you plan to do.

LOVER See *Meeting*.

LUNATIC ASYLUM To be locked up in an asylum means you are not understood by your associates and have difficulties explaining yourself. To see others locked up means you need to take great care in expressing yourself or you will be misunderstood. To see someone you know locked up means you are worried about a friend. (Also see *Madness*.)

MACARONI See *Eating / Drinking*.

MACKEREL To dream of fishing for mackerel is a sure sign that you will be traveling in the near future. To dream of eating mackerel signifies that someone will be coming to visit you.

MADNESS To dream of being mad shows a feeling of restriction; of being unable to express yourself. (Also see *Lunatic Asylum*.)

MAGAZINE To dream you are reading a magazine means that if you apply yourself you will make great advances. To see a magazine rack, or someone else reading a magazine, means that you will come into contact with someone who is able to help you advance.

MAGISTRATE You have made some error, of which you are not aware. Go back over your previous day's work and double-check everything.

MAGNIFYING GLASS To dream that you are looking at things through a magnifying glass means that you have overextended yourself financially.

MAID To see a serving maid means that you will receive some good news. If you are the maid, then you will get bad news.

MAIL See *Letter*.

MAIL CARRIER To see a mail carrier means that you will be negotiating with a salesperson. If you are the mail carrier, it means you have been overcharged for something you recently bought.

MANDOLIN To see and hear a mandolin being played means you will enjoy an intimate, romantic time with someone for whom you care.

MANSION Signifies that you feel you are worth far more than you are receiving. Try to better your position by asking either for a raise or for promotion.

MARBLES Playing marbles means that you will visit someone you knew many years ago. If you watch others playing marbles then you will be visited by someone from the past.

MARE See *Horse*.

MARIONETTES If you dream that you are a marionette, you are being manipulated. If you watch a marionette show, you are aware of the manipulation of someone else.

MARRIAGE See *Wedding*.

MATCHES To see a number of matches means you will have many close friends (only one match—only one close friend). To strike a match presages the start of a new and exciting friendship. To blow out a match is the end of a long-standing friendship.

MATTRESS Any problems you are presently going through will come to a speedy conclusion. You will soon be able to relax again.

MAYOR See *Meeting*.

MAYPOLE Dreaming of dancing around a Maypole is a sure sign of being in love.

MEAT See *Eating/Drinking*.

MEDALS To be awarded a medal, or to be

wearing one, means that you will receive recognition for an accomplishment. To see someone else wearing a medal means you must try to curb feelings of jealousy.

MEETING In many dreams you meet with different types of people. Here are the meanings for some that can be significant. See, also, separate headings for some of these.

MEETING WITH:

Baker Symbolizes gain.

Beggar Unexpected help from an unlikely source.

Blind Person You have false friends.

Brigand Fear, deep down inside.

Cardinal You will have to relocate against your will.

Child You will experience difficulties in business.

Doctor You are a person of honor and will be recognized as such.

Dwarf Great danger lies ahead.

Footman Enemies. You will undertake a journey that could be very dangerous.

Grandparent A legacy.

Hangman The Gypsies say that to see a hangman in your dreams means you will meet with a premature death.

Hermit A treacherous friend.

Horseman Pride.

Judge Punishment. (See also *Magistrate*, separate listing.)

Laborer Conjugal happiness and increase of fortune.

Lady/Lord Humiliation.

Lame Person Misfortunes in business.

Lawyer A friend's marriage.

Locksmith Robbery.

Lover Trouble; disputes.

Mayor Malice.

Millionaire You will collect on money owed to you from the past; money you had forgotten about.

Moneylender Persecution.

Nurse Long life.

Old Man/Woman You will be called upon to display your knowledge to others.

Pageboy/Valet Abuse of confidence.

Painter Long, happy life.

Pilgrim You will be justly rewarded.

Police Officer Apprehension.

Priest Scandal.

Prince Honor and profit.

Queen Prosperity.

Rival Family quarrels.

Sailor Tidings from across the sea.

Sculptor Profit from hard work.

Secretary Assistance coming.

Shepherd You will be asked to take on extra responsibilities.

Soldier Quarrels.

Tailor Infidelity.

Uncle Advantages.

Waiter/Waitress Suspicion.

Woodcutter Hard work for no return.

MELONS See *Fruits*.

MERMAID You will have great expectations followed by big disappointments.

MERRY-GO-ROUND See *Carousel*.

MILITARY OFFICER See *Colonel*.

MILK/MILKING To dream of drinking milk indicates you will be very lucky in love. To dream of milking a cow means you will have to work at winning the person you desire, but you will eventually be successful.

MILLET See *Eating/Drinking*.

MILLIONAIRE Financial success. If you are the millionaire, you will soon be in a position to help others. (See also *Meeting*.)

MIRROR Betrayal by a friend. A broken mirror signifies that you will be the one betraying a friend.

MISER If you see a miser counting his or her gold, it's the best dream you can have, say the Gypsies. It means you will become rich and prosperous and have a full and happy life.

MIST See *Fog*.

MISTLETOE If you dream that you are being kissed under the mistletoe at Christmas, that person will become very important in your life when you actually are kissed under such circumstances. If you dream of a bough of mistletoe falling, it means that you will never marry or, if already married, that you will divorce. If you dream of cutting mistletoe from a tree, then you will have your choice of lovers.

MONASTERY See *Abbey*.

MONEY To give money away means you will lose money in business. To find money means you will have to borrow from others. To receive money, as a gift or in payment, means you will receive fair recompense for services.

MONEYLENDER See *Meeting*.

MONKEY See *Ape*.

MOON The moon is tied in with luck and love. To see a full moon means you will be blessed; a new moon means a wish will be granted. A partially clouded moon means you will be lucky in love. To see a moon reflected in water means you will have great expectations but be disappointed in love. (Interestingly, the Romani word *moon* means "month.")

MOSS Dreaming of soft, green moss indicates that you are of a loving nature; very affectionate.

MOUNTAIN You have lofty aspirations. If you work hard towards your goal you can achieve it and rise to an important position.

MOURNING To dream of being in mourning

is a reversal of what will actually happen. It means that you will soon have cause for great celebration.

MOUSE/MICE Dreaming of mice generally means you will experience small, petty annoyances. If you are frightened by a mouse then you will be very embarrassed over some incident. To see a mouse being chased is a sure sign that you do not stand up for yourself; you let other people push you around. To catch a mouse means you will receive an unpleasant letter. A mouse already caught in a trap is recognition that you have been made to do something you didn't want to do.

MUD This is a symbol of evil that is being directed at you. If you are spattered with mud, people are maligning you. If you walk or drive through mud, you will come into contact with people who will speak ill of you.

MUFF See *Dress*.

MULE See *Ass / Donkey*.

MURDER If you dream of being accused of murder, you will get into an argument with your friends. If you commit a murder, you are refusing to face facts and will get into a difficult situation because of it.

MUSTARD See *Eating/Drinking*.

NAKED See *Bare/Naked*.

NAPKIN A fine white napkin indicates that you have a true and faithful friend who will do anything for you. If you drop a napkin, you will do something to hurt that friendship.

NECKLACE To be wearing an especially

fine necklace means that you will be taking part in an important social event. A small, insignificant necklace can mean jealousy and petty annoyances.

NEEDLES See *Dress*.

NEGLIGEE For a woman to dream that she is dressed in nothing but her negligee means that she has a secret that she is fearful of having discovered.

NEWSPAPER To buy a newspaper means that you will receive a letter. To be reading a newspaper means that you will get news that could be good or bad, but is more likely to be bad.

NEW YEAR The Gypsies say that to dream of any aspect of a new year—a New Year's Eve party, being wished a happy new year, etc.—indicates that you will have a chance to start afresh, start a new project, implement new ideas, change your course of action, etc.

NIGHTINGALE To hear or see a nightingale is the forerunner of joyful news, great success in business, joy in love.

NOVEL See *Library*.

NUDE See *Bare/Naked*.

NUMBERS Numbers appearing in dreams are important and you should try hard to remember them, especially if several numbers come together (see Chapter 7, "Dreaming For Profit"). The meanings and associations of individual numbers are as follows:

Zero Harmony; unity.

One Solitude; loneliness.

Two Happiness; the perfect couple.

Three Dispute; arguments.

Four Choices; decisions.

Five Balance.

Six Exploration; outgoing.

Seven Luck and blessings.

Eight New beginnings; new life.

Nine Family and children.

NUN/NUNNERY Beware of false friends.

NURSE You are tired of responsibilities; you need assistance in your business and/or private life. (See also *Meeting*.)

NUTS See *Fruits*.

OAK TREE Symbolizes a good, solid marriage. If acorns are falling, or have fallen, from it then the marriage will bring many children.

OAR To be rowing with two oars means you will forge ahead due to your own efforts. To lose an oar while rowing means you will suffer a minor setback but will quickly recover.

OATS A sign of stability and basic success. You will have a firm footing, with a solid business backing.

OBITUARY To see or read an obituary means a close friend will relocate far away. To read your own obituary means you will be the one relocating.

OFFICERS Any sort of officer, whether of the law or the armed services, indicates trouble. You will have a brush with the law, or experience trouble through some technicalities, due either to something you have overlooked or something of which you were ignorant. (See also *Colonel / Military Officer*.)

OIL Generally associated with wealth. To see an oil field signifies that you have money coming. To use an oilcan, buy oil, or pour oil, means you will be well rewarded for your efforts. To spill oil is to lose money.

OLD MAN/WOMAN See *Meeting*.

OLIVES See *Fruits*.

ONIONS Different Gypsies have varied things to say about onions. Generally they tie in with luck, be it good or bad. If you dream of eating onions, some say you will be a receiver of stolen property while others say you will discover some hidden treasure. However, many Gypsies say that eating onions means you will get into a very disagreeable argument, perhaps with your own family. To throw away onions means you will break up with your spouse or lover. If you buy onions you will receive an unexpected bonus.

OPERA Symbolizes pleasure followed by unhappiness.

OPULENCE Symbolizes extravagance on your part. Be careful or you will overspend.

ORANGE See *Colors*.

ORANGE BLOSSOM There is peace and tranquillity to come . . . but it may not last.

ORANGES See *Fruits*.

ORATION See *Speech*.

ORCHARD To dream that you are in an orchard, according to the Gypsies, either means that you will become rich by inheriting a legacy, or that you will marry someone wealthy. For a married person to dream of being in an orchard means there will be many children who, in their turn, will become very wealthy.

ORGAN To hear organ music, or see someone playing the organ, means that you will receive very good news. But if the chords should happen to be discordant then you will receive very bad news.

ORGAN GRINDER / HURDY-GURDY To see an organ grinder and/or listen to his or her music indicates that you are being manipulated by someone. If you are working the hurdy-gurdy, you are the manipulator.

OSTRICH FEATHERS A large number of ostrich feathers is a sign of prosperity, say the Rom, but this is not necessarily accompanied by happiness.

OVEN An oven or cooking stove indicates that you will be relocating; moving to a larger home.

OWL See *Birds*.

OXEN To see an ox, or a yoke of oxen, signifies that you will have a hard life with little reward for your pains.

OYSTERS See *Eating/Drinking*.

PAGEBOY See *Meeting*.

PAINT To dream of painting a house, or putting a fresh coat of paint on anything, signifies that you have something to hide; something you are trying to cover up. If someone else is doing the painting, then a friend or associate is hiding something from you.

PAINTER See *Meeting*.

PAINTINGS To see and/or admire fine paintings means that you have many false friends and that you are wasting a great deal of time.

PALACE A dream of a palace portends a raising of your standards of living. Beware of living beyond your means.

PALM READER See *Fortuneteller*.

PALM TREE There will be recognition for work you have done and services rendered. The palm tree is a symbol of honor and victory.

PANCAKE Seeing, cooking, or eating pancakes means that some of the things which you presently think of as curses in your life are going to turn out to be blessings.

PARADISE To find yourself in what appears to be Paradise means you are not being realistic about your work and your surroundings.

PARASOL To carry a parasol shows that you have many good, close friends. To open a parasol is to receive surprise gifts or advice from these friends.

PARROT See *Birds*.

PASTRY See *Eating/Drinking*.

PATCHWORK See *Quilt*.

PAWNSHOP You are going to be exchanging one set of problems for another.

PEACHES See *Fruits*.

PEACOCK See *Birds*.

PEARLS See *Dress*.

PEARS See *Fruits*.

PEN/PENCIL You will be in a position to make a choice which will affect a large number of people.

PEPPERMINT You will be left a sum of money by a distant relative.

PERFUME If you smell perfume, or apply perfume, you will have a date with a very attractive member of the opposite sex. You will think about becoming romantically involved with him or her.

PHOTOGRAPH If you dream that you are looking at a photograph of yourself it is a sign that you will become ill. To look at a photograph of someone else indicates jealousy on your part.

PIANO To see and hear the piano being played indicates that you will be going to a party. If you are playing the piano, you will be throwing the party.

PICKPOCKET To dream of a pickpocket shows a need for you to obtain information you are having difficulty getting. If you are the pickpocket, you are willing to obtain this information illegally if necessary.

PICNIC You will have a good time with close friends, though there may be a few petty arguments.

PIG You are assured of success. This is a good time for investing. Whatever you turn your hand to will prosper.

PIGEON See *Birds*.

PILGRIM See *Meeting*.

PIMPLES To find your face covered with pimples means that others are very jealous of you.

PINE TREE Symbolizes an exciting but possibly dangerous exploit. It could even be an exciting date . . . one you could live to regret.

PINS See *Dress*.

PIPE See *Smoke*.

PIRATE You are going to be doing a lot of traveling. Beware of accidents.

PISTOL/REVOLVER You have an explosive temper. Be careful or you could say something that will hurt someone and that you will very much regret. (See also *Gun*.)

PIT See *Hole*.

PITCHFORK The Gypsies say that a pitchfork is a sign of excellent health. If you are using a pitchfork you will be very healthy. If you are chased by someone with a pitchfork, you need to pay more attention to your health.

PLOW Concentrate on doing your best. Hard work now will lead to great success in the future. This applies both to business and to home life.

PLUMS See *Fruits*.

POCKETBOOK/PURSE To dream of losing a pocketbook means that you are frequently careless and disorganized. To find a pocketbook means that you will have unexpected good fortune.

POLICE To be arrested by a police officer, or *gavmush*, means you will do something that will necessitate your apologizing to friends. To talk with a police officer means that you are in need of advice. (See also *Meeting*.)

POMEGRANATE See *Fruits*.

PONY See *Horse*.

POOL See *Billiards*.

POPE To dream of the Pope indicates extravagance. If you dream that you are the Pope then you have been overspending foolishly.

POPPIES A field of poppies is a sign of adventures in love.

PORCUPINE/HEDGEHOG Indicates business embarrassments, though some Gypsies say it means a better job but disappointment in friends.

PORT/DOCK Symbolizes a home/focal point. If you dream of arriving at a dock you will be going home. To see a ship steam into port similarly indicates that you will be going home, or to the place where you feel most comfortable.

POSTCARD You will be attending a social event at which you will be very unsure of yourself.

POST OFFICE You will be meeting with a great many strangers.

POWDER FLASK Go cautiously, there is some danger should you make the wrong move. (See also *Gunpowder*.)

PREACHER You will encounter a con artist.

PRECIPICE You have a big decision to make. Should you fall down a precipice, you have made a wrong decision!

PRIEST See *Preacher* and *Meeting*.

PRINCE See *Meeting*.

PRINTER You are very much admired for your intelligence and your ease of communication.

PRISON See *Jail*.

PROCESSION Symbolizes constancy in love.

PUMP To be at a pump drawing water means that you will have good fortune in business; money flowing in. If, however, you are pumping and can get no water out, then you will have a failure in your business dealings.

PURPLE See *Colors*.

PURSE See *Pocketbook*.

QUARREL To dream that you are quarreling with someone signifies that you will have advantageous dealings with a business associate. To dream of quarreling with your lover means you will actually draw even closer and will receive a gift from him or her.

QUEEN See *Meeting*.

QUILT To see or handle a quilt is a good sign for financial advances. To be making a quilt shows that you will get good return for the work you have done. A patchwork quilt is a sign of flattery and gossip, say the Gypsies. Take all you hear with a grain of salt and don't be easily swayed.

RABBIT See *Hare*.

RACING To dream of running a race shows disappointment and anger, especially with your lover. To dream you are riding in a horse race is a good sign and presages much success in life; you will speedily receive some joyful news, possibly from your lover.

RAGS To see someone dressed in rags means you have been unfair to someone you really care about. To see yourself dressed in rags means you will come into an inheritance. To dream of handling cleaning rags means you will make money through your own hard work.

RAILROAD Signifies security in the long run. You will make slow but steady progress.

RAILROAD ACCIDENT Your plans will go awry. There will be unexpected pitfalls that will "throw you off the tracks."

RAIN A gentle shower of rain shows success in your present undertakings. It is an especially good sign for lovers. But if it is heavy rain, with occasional flashes of lightning and rolls of thunder, then beware for there are going to be many problems and discouragements. (See also *Lightning* and *Thunder and Lightning*.)

RAINBOW Gypsies believe that if you see a rainbow in your dreams great happiness will come to you unexpectedly—frequently taking place in the area of love.

RAKE To dream of a garden rake indicates that you need to get your plans better organized. You cannot progress until you have a clearer understanding of where you want to go.

RAM This animal indicates that you are trying to force the issue. You need to relax and let things move under their own steam for a while.

RAT You have a secret enemy who is working against you. Someone who appears to be a friend (though not a close one) is really an enemy. He or she is not so much plotting against you but is learning your secrets to use to his or her advantage.

RAVEN See *Birds*.

REAPER See *Scythe*.

RED See *Colors*.

REPTILE Someone you are not sure about is

actually a very good friend who will work for your well-being. Given recognition, this person will turn out to be the best friend you have ever had.

RETIREMENT To dream of retiring indicates a need for a vacation. You have been working for too long without a break. Give yourself a well-deserved rest.

REVOLVER See *Pistol*.

RIBBONS See *Dress*.

RICE See *Eating / Drinking*.

RIDING To dream of going horseback riding means that you will enjoy pleasure at the price of your good name.

RING See *Dress*.

RIOT To dream that you witness, or are engaged in, a riot means that you will get unexpected news and an unexpected visitor. It can also mean that the object of your affections is wavering between you and another suitor.

RIVAL See *Meeting*.

RIVER To dream you see a flowing river whose waters are smooth and clear presages happiness and success in life; for the married person, contentment in family life. If the waters of the river are rough and muddy, you will be taking a journey that could lead to an increase in your fortunes, though there are certain risks attached.

ROAD The Rom say that a wide, straight road indicates you will find things coming to you very easily, without too much effort on your part. If the road is winding, with ups and downs, then that is how you will find life: many ups and downs and changes of fortune along the way.

ROAST See *Eating/Drinking*.

ROCK An obstruction; an annoyance. Note how you get around, or over, the rock in your dream. A falling rock indicates an unexpected change of fortune.

ROCKING CHAIR To see someone, or yourself, rocking in a chair is a sign that you will have an easy, contented life. To rock an empty chair means that there will be many hard times.

ROPE To see and/or handle rope signifies

you will be in a position to make several very useful friends. If there are knots in the rope you will have a few problems but will overcome them. If you cut a rope you will sever what could be a very useful relationship.

ROSE Always a happy omen, according to the Gypsies. A full-bloom rose indicates health, joy and happiness. A rosebud signifies the potential for a wonderful friendship to develop. A faded rose means you are neglecting an old friend. A white rose shows innocence; a red rose, satisfaction.

RUBY Strong, romantic love, though it may be fleeting.

RUG See *Carpet*.

RUNNING To be running in your dream means that time is passing and you need to act quickly or you will miss an opportunity.

SADDLE You will have ease and comfort in life.

SAILOR Indicative of journeys. You may be relocating or it may just be a journey away and back home again. (See also *Meeting*.)

SALAD See *Eating/Drinking*.

SALMON A sign of deceit. To eat salmon means you will discover the deceiver.

SALT See *Eating/Drinking*.

SAND Indicates a coming increase in finances. Investments will bring good returns, but beware that new-found money is not as quickly washed away again.

SANDALS To be wearing sandals is a sign of success. If the sandals hurt your feet, you will have many problems but will eventually overcome them all.

SASH To be wearing a sash means that you will be singled out for some sort of recognition, but that it will cause jealousy among your friends.

SATIN See *Dress*.

SAUSAGES See *Eating/Drinking*.

SCARAB The Egyptian scarab is a sacred beetle and in a dream indicates that you are on the right path. If you continue working as industriously as you have been it will lead to rich rewards.

SCARE To dream you are scared by some frightening object or event shows that you have many reservations about a decision you have recently made. You need to examine that decision.

SCISSORS See *Dress*.

SCULPTOR See *Meeting*.

SCYTHE Gypsy dream symbol for cutting back or ending. If you are the one with the scythe then you feel the need to cut back on something, or put an end to an action or situation. If you see the "Grim Reaper"—an often robed skeletal figure with a scythe—it does not necessarily mean death. It could indicate a death to come, but it could just as easily indicate the coming end of a job, situation, relationship, or whatever. Don't forget that where there are endings there are, necessarily, new beginnings and therefore new opportunities.

SEA A long journey. A calm sea means that it will be a successful and enjoyable journey. A rough sea indicates many problems and worries.

SEAL A single seal or a group of seals indicates that you will be going on a fishing trip.

SEALING WAX You will receive the approval you have been waiting for, to go ahead with what you have planned.

SEAWEED Someone is trying to prevent you from taking a journey that would prove beneficial for you.

SECRETARY See *Meeting*.

SERMON If you are listening to a sermon you will receive some good advice from a friend. You will be wise to follow it. If you are delivering a sermon you will be accused of double-crossing someone.

SERPENT See *Reptile*.

SHADOWS Strong shadows in your dreams indicate pessimism and the possibility of failure, say the Gypsies. However bright your prospects seem you will still be conscious of the fact that things could go terribly wrong.

SHAMROCK You will have a wonderful time with someone you admire very much.

SHARK Danger from jealous enemies. Do not be panicked into doing anything without careful thought.

SHAVING To dream of shaving means you tend to be miserly. To cut yourself while shaving means you are going to lose money through your unwillingness to speculate.

SHAWL Gypsies say it symbolizes solace and comfort.

SHEEP Slow and steady progress. To shear a sheep means a profit in business. Herding sheep means you are worried about a close friend's actions.

SHEPHERD See *Meeting*.

SHERIFF See *Bailiff*.

SHIP See *Boat*.

SHIPWRECK You will suffer a dangerous illness but it will not prove fatal.

SHIRT To take off a shirt means you will lose a friend. To lose a button off a shirt means petty squabbles. To wear a bright, clean shirt means happiness to come.

SHOES See *Boots*.

SHOOTING To dream of shooting means you are ready to act, to go ahead with something you have been brooding about for a long time. To hunt and shoot with bow and arrow means you will be taking a big chance, but the risk could pay off very well. (See also *Arrow*.)

SILK See *Dress*.

SILVER Silver money and ingots indicate honors and prestige that will come to you. The

Rom say that to dream of silverware on a dining table means you will receive unwelcome visitors in your home.

SINGING To be singing with others means you will enjoy meeting with old friends. To sing solo means you will find yourself alone.

SKELETON You will be involved in some unusual activities. (Skeleton with a scythe, see *Scythe*.)

SKULL You will make a big discovery that could greatly benefit you.

SMOKE If you see smoke, from a chimney or fire, you will enjoy a brief moment of joy but it will not last. To smoke a cigarette or pipe indicates you have great confidence in yourself, which may or may not be justified. (See also *Chimney*.)

SNAIL You seem to be making slow and steady progress but if you stop to examine things you will find you are going in the wrong direction.

SNAKE See *Reptile*.

SNOW Light snow falling is a sign of contentment. Heavy snow is a warning to exercise caution. To see snow weighting down branches of trees means you are under pressure to produce. Children playing in the snow means you will be justly rewarded.

SOLDIER Be prepared for troubles to come. To see a number of soldiers means more and bigger troubles. (See also *Meeting*.)

SOUP See *Eating/Drinking*.

SPEECH To be listening to a speech means that you will shortly have an opportunity to learn things which can be of great benefit to you. If you are delivering a speech, you will be in a position to help someone who will appreciate your assistance.

SPIDER To dream of spiders is lucky. They symbolize luck and great prosperity through industry. You will soon achieve your ambition. If the spider is on a web then the good fortune will come from a number of different sources.

SQUIRREL A squirrel storing nuts means that you will enjoy social success. But a squirrel chasing through the branches of a tree means debtors will be after you.

STAG Represents eventual financial and

social gain. To see a stag killed means there will be a scandal. If you are the one who kills the stag, you will be the center of a scandal. (See also *Deer*.)

STARS Bright stars in the sky mean recovery from an illness. A shooting star signifies the birth of a baby.

STEAMBOAT Unexpected news from afar.

STEEPLE You will meet an interesting person of the opposite sex. Carefully check out him or her before becoming involved.

STORK Foretells a robbery.

STRAWBERRIES See *Fruits*.

STREAM See *Brook*.

SUNRISE/SET A beautiful sunrise presages success in a new venture. A beautiful sunset tells of rewards to come from work already done.

SWALLOW See *Birds*.

SWAN You will have a happy and contented family life. If there are cygnets with the swan(s), then you will have children.

SWEEP (CHIMNEY) You will acquire a store of very useful knowledge—a piece here, a piece there—which you will suddenly realize can be put together and used for your profit.

SWEEPING Gypsies in the southwest of England claim that to be sweeping with a broom means that you need to clear out all the smaller, accumulated bits and pieces of your life and concentrate on the more important things.

SWIMMING To dream of swimming with your head above water means you will have good success. To swim with your head under the water means you will be weighted down with problems. To swim in the nude means you will enjoy social successes.

SWORD To hold a sword, wear one, or brandish one means you will be awarded some special recognition. To be fighting with a sword means you will quarrel with business associates.

SYCAMORE To dream of the sycamore tree means there is jealousy in your marriage or love affair.

TAILOR You are going to be very busy with little time to enjoy yourself. (See also *Meeting*.)

TAMBOURINE If you play a tambourine you are going to be held accountable for your actions... and are not too happy at the prospects! If you watch someone else playing a tambourine, you will be in a position to call on others to account for their actions.

TANDEM To dream of a tandem bicycle means you will be going into partnership, either in business or by getting married.

TATTOO You will never be able to keep any secret to yourself.

TAXI See *Cab*.

TEA If you dream that you are pouring tea for someone it means you will be approached for a loan. To dream of drinking tea with someone is a sign that that person is good and trustworthy.

TEARS To dream that you are in tears means that you will receive a letter containing bad news. If you see a baby crying it is a sign that the letter will have good news.

TELESCOPE You will be traveling to a distant place that you will find interesting and exciting.

TENT A Gypsy tent is known as a *bender*. To dream of sleeping in a tent is to feel safe and secure. To dream that you are erecting a tent means you are working well towards your own security.

THEATRE To be at a theatre, or moviehouse, or watching a play, means you will attend a social event but will feel out of place there.

THIRST To dream you have an unquenchable thirst signifies that you seek new knowledge; you are looking for an answer to a long-term problem.

THISTLE You are attracted to someone who could hurt you, though not seriously.

THORNS Gypsies say that dreaming of thorns mean you are stepping on dangerous ground. You could suffer greatly if you rush on without thinking of where you are going, so plan ahead as thoroughly and carefully as you can.

THUNDER AND LIGHTNING Rough times ahead with much dispute, arguments, disagreement, possibly even law suits. If you hear thunder without seeing lightning, then you will come out of it all right. (See also *Lightning*.)

TIGER Fierce enmity; animosity towards a particular person. To hunt a tiger means that a trap has been laid for you but you will recognize it and avoid it. To kill a tiger means triumph over your enemies.

TINKER To dream that you are a tinker, mending pots and pans, means that you will be prosperous in business, successful as a lover, and happy and contented when married.

TOAD To dream of a toad indicates the possibility of an accident. To pick up a toad means a minor aggravation, such as a cut finger or stubbed toe.

TOMB To enter a tomb means you will suffer an illness. To be locked in a tomb means it will be a very serious illness.

TORCH To dream of carrying a lighted torch symbolizes troubles to come in your love life. To extinguish a torch means you will break with your present lover.

TORTOISE See *Turtle*.

TRAIN To see a train going by is a sign of missed opportunity. To be riding on a train means you will achieve goals even though you don't work especially hard towards them. A freight train is indicative of manual labor, while a passenger train points to mental work. (See also *Engine*.)

TRAMP See *Hobo*.

TRAVELING Frequently symbolizes spiritual progression, though the Gypsies are usually not especially aware of this. To them to dream of traveling, in whatever form, is a natural progression of life; advancement, goals attained, new friends and situations.

TRAY To dream of holding a tray indicates that you will be supporting someone, either financially or morally. To drop a tray is to let down a friend.

TREASURE To hunt for treasure is to seek recognition. To discover buried or sunken treasure is to receive an unexpected award or recognition.

TREE A tree symbolizes strength and beauty

to the Gypsies. To see a number of trees, or a wood, is to know that you will have many children who will grow up tall and strong. To dream of cutting down a tree means that you will harm yourself. To see a leafless tree means you will suffer sickness. Climbing a tree signifies excelling in your field. To break a branch from a tree is a falling-out with your lover. (See, also, individual tree names.)

TRIPLETS A sign of good luck, health, wealth, and abundance.

TROMBONE To play a trombone, see or hear one being played, signifies success in love.

TRUMPET To play a trumpet, see or hear one being played, signifies a mild flirtation which could develop into something serious.

TULIPS To dream of these flowers is a sign of abundance. If you see yourself standing in a garden surrounded by tulips, it foretells that you will be rich and distinguished.

TUNNEL To dream of going through a lighted tunnel denotes that you will successfully negotiate your way through one or more difficult times—possibly business dealings, or domestic problems. Going through a dark tunnel means you will have a really hard time along the way.

TURKEY A live turkey means you will be asked to make a speech. A dead, or cooked, turkey forebodes involvement in a scandal.

TURNIP To dream of being in a turnip field denotes acquisition of riches; to the lover they augur great fidelity and good temper in your sweetheart.

TURTLE/TORTOISE Symbolizes delays and vexations in business affairs.

ULCERS To dream you have ulcers is to acknowledge that you are greatly concerned about something; worrying more than you should. Try to relax and bring your worries and fears out into the open or you may well develop real ulcers.

UMBRELLA Carrying an umbrella in your dreams indicates that you feel vulnerable and in need of protection. This is doubly so if you have an open umbrella.

UNCLE/AUNT To see them in your dreams is a sign of upcoming family quarrels. (See also *Meeting*.)

UNDERCLOTHING To dream you are not wearing underwear means you are afraid of being found out in a lie; you have something to hide. To be wearing torn underclothing means you are ashamed of some recent action of yours.

UNDERTAKER The Rom say that to meet with an undertaker in your dreams is to anticipate such a meeting in real life. Someone you know, but not a relative, will soon die and you will attend the funeral.

URGENCY If there is great urgency in your, or someone else's, actions in your dream it is a sign that you are very impatient.

VALET See *Meeting*.

VALLEY All Gypsies seem to agree that to be walking in a valley is a sign of contentment and tranquillity, and a knowledge of protection.

VARDO See *Carriage*.

VAULT A bank vault is a sign of hidden riches. You are trying to obtain something but are frustrated in its acquisition. A bank vault with an open door is a sign that you are giving away too many secrets; talking too much.

VEIL See *Dress*.

VELVET The Gypsies say that to dream of black velvet is a portent of a coming death. Purple velvet signifies glory and luxury to come. Red velvet is a dangerous affair that could lead to scandal. Blue velvet is a need for a vacation. Green velvet is a sign of unexpected wealth.

VENUS For a young man to dream of the Goddess Venus signifies that he is seeking the ideal woman. For a young woman to dream of the Lady means she is feeling sexually frustrated.

VINEGAR See *Eating/Drinking*.

VINEYARD A full vineyard, with many bunches of rich purple grapes, symbolizes a life of riches and good fortune. Green, unripe grapes on the vines indicate the potential for riches but you will have to work at it.

VIOLIN The *bosh* is a favorite instrument of

the Gypsies. To dream that you see and/or hear one being played is a very good sign, symbolizing much enjoyment and good company. To dream that you are the one playing it is to know that you are much loved and admired.

VIRGIN For a woman to dream she is a virgin is to wish to be desirable to men. For a man to dream of a virgin is to desire a younger woman.

VIXEN A vixen is a symbol for a mixture of beauty and cunning. Beware of any especially beautiful, self-assured woman who seems to attract you.

VULTURE See *Birds*.

WAGGON See *Carriage*.

WAITER/WAITRESS See *Meeting*.

WAR To dream of a war being fought

indicates that there will be a great scandal in which you will play a prominent part!

WARMING PAN To dream of a warming pan indicates that you will be going to bed with a stranger.

WASP Wasps are signs of trouble with envious people. To be stung by a wasp means you will spend money foolishly.

WATCH To be wearing a watch, or to consult a watch, in your dreams means you will be visited by a very important person.

WATER Clear, cold water is a sign of good health. Warm or dirty water indicates illness. To empty water out of a vessel shows you have an unhealthy appetite and need to watch what you eat.

WATERFALL A sign that you will meet with many new and interesting people who will like you.

WATER MILL You will have continuing good health and a steady income, with little change over many years.

WEALTH What you dream you have in wealth, you lack in health, say the Gypsies. If you dream you are very rich then you need to pay a lot of attention to your health.

WEASEL Cunning and deceit.

WEDDING Attending a wedding means you will meet new friends. If it is your own wedding, you will be extremely fortunate in love.

WEEDS To see a garden filled with weeds means that you need to review your diet and health, for if you continue as you are you will become extremely ill.

WEEPING See *Tears*.

WELL To draw water from a well means that

you will meet with a stranger who will provide you with much useful information.

WHEAT A field of ripe wheat indicates that you will grow rich. If the wheat has already been harvested, you will just miss a wonderful opportunity to make a lot of money (such as being close to the winning number in a lottery).

WHEELS Turning wheels emphasized in a dream indicate travel. If the wheels are stationary you will be making some short trips.

WHIP To use a whip, or see a whip being used, indicates that you have a short temper and sharp tongue that can hurt others more than you realize.

WHIRLPOOL You are in a very dangerous situation and could be swept away, without warning, at any time.

WHIRLWIND You will get into a tremendous argument with a relative and say things which you will later regret.

WHITE DRESS To dream of a woman in a white dress or to dream of wearing a white dress portends that you will be accused of some malicious gossip but will be proven innocent.

WIDOW For a woman to dream that she is a widow means that her lover is being unfaithful.

WIG To dream of wearing a wig means you are being pretentious or allowing people to believe things about you which are not true.

WILL To dream that you are writing your will means that you are very dissatisfied with the actions of some close relative(s).

WINDMILL If the sails of the windmill are turning then you will enjoy a large inheritance. If they are at a standstill then the inheritance will be small.

WINE To dream that you are drinking wine is a good omen, say the Gypsies. It prognosticates health, wealth, long life and happiness. If you are in love you will marry the person you adore. If you are married, you will draw especially close to your spouse.

WOLF Symbolizes strength and independence.

WOOD See *Tree*.

WOODCUTTER See *Meeting*.

WORM To dream of worms is a warning that you may be in contact with someone who has a contagious disease.

WRECK A wreck at sea is a sign of a tedious and costly lawsuit, which could lead to poverty and even imprisonment.

WRITING DESK To be sitting at a writing desk signifies that your words will carry a lot of weight; what you say will have an effect on many people.

YACHT To see a yacht go sailing by means you will become friendly with a person who is wealthy. If you are sailing the yacht, you will become wealthy yourself.

YARN A ball of yarn signals the start of a long, winding affair, either business or of the heart.

YELLOW See *Colors*.

YEW TREE A symbol of strength. You are someone others can lean on when they have a need. Your friends find that they can turn to you with their problems.

YOKE See *Oxen*.

ZEBRA Some Gypsies say this indicates misplaced friendship. Others say it simply means there are two equally important sides to a problem under consideration; either choice could be right.

ZODIAC To dream of the zodiac as a whole shows a great interest in your fellow humans; an inquiring and active mind. To dream of any particular sign, you must consider the general astrological meanings. The common Romani interpretations are as follows:

Aries Leader; pioneer. Sometimes impatient and overly ambitious.

Taurus Hard worker. Great strength (and proud of it); perseverance.

Gemini Adaptable. Knows a little about a lot of things. Gift for languages.

Cancer Extremely sensitive. Home-lover. Follower of tradition.

Leo Extrovert. Sense of the dramatic. Great lover.

Virgo Conservative. Critical; analytical. Best of planners/organizers. Intellectual.

Libra Has intuition and foresight. Peace-loving, with great sense of justice.

Scorpio Has tenacity and determination. Great self-control but too fine an opinion of self. Can be jealous and demanding.

Sagittarius Knows no fear. Kind and gentle, yet outspoken and direct.

Capricorn Ambitious; materialistic. Fear of inadequacy. Can be greatly depressed or incredibly happy.

Aquarius The planner. Always looking ahead. Independent. Honest and kind but difficult to understand.

Pisces Sensitive; noble. Can be vague and overly optimistic. Excellent diplomat.

The Gypsies connect the parts of the body with the signs as follows:

Head: Aries

Neck: Taurus

Arms: Gemini

Heart: Leo

Breast: Cancer

Kidneys: Libra

Bowels: Virgo

Genitalia: Scorpio

Thighs: Sagittarius

Legs: Aquarius

Knees: Capricorn

Feet: Pisces

So if you dream of, for example, the zodiacal sign Capricorn, it could be because of a problem you have with your knee(s) and/or indicative of feelings of inadequacy.

4
Dream Interpretation

In order to read the true meaning of your dreams you must study the component parts and how they relate to one another. You can't just consider one thing and ignore everything else. By the same token, not everything in your dream is significant. For instance, if you dream you enter a room and, looking around, see everything in the room—chairs, table, bookcase, pictures on the wall, furnishings and decorations—not every single item is significant and needs to be interpreted. This is the problem with many dream books that give explanations of 1,000, 10,000, 50,000, or however many dream symbols! You can get so wrapped up in checking everything you remember that you lose the main message of the dream. All you need check are the major components: those that strike you particularly; those that really stand out. Also study the people in the dream and how they relate to you.

Generally the *main character* in a dream—whoever it happens to be—represents *you*. Let's say that you dream of your Uncle Charlie (someone you always liked and admired) and see him doing something he shouldn't be doing. For example, let's say he is drinking beer and smoking cigarettes; something he doesn't normally do. In fact "Uncle Charlie," in the dream, is you. Your unconscious mind knows that to show you yourself drinking and smoking would have little effect on you, since it is something you do on a regular basis. But to show your favorite uncle doing it, when he doesn't normally, will have a strong impact on you and, consequently, perhaps make you break these habits.

As another example, you might dream that your little sister is using a long rawhide whip and is whipping people standing about her! This doesn't make sense since your sister is a mild little thing, full of love for everyone. But the universal symbolism of a whip is a sharp tongue and bad temper; something that can really hurt people. In the dream your sister represents yourself; again to make a bigger impact on you. What your unconscious mind is doing, then, is pointing out to you that your bad temper and sharp tongue can hurt others and you should do something about it.

So the first thing to remember, in interpreting your dreams, is that not everyone is who they seem to be. So far as the main characters in the dream are concerned, they (one *or more* of them) just might be representing you. Look at the dream from that possibility first, to see if it makes sense. Study it to see if there are any other clues to the fact that it is you shown there.

Let's now look at a longer, more complicated dream, in which you were shown as yourself. Suppose you were able to remember all, or most, of the details of a dream which seemed just an ordinary one about a walk in the country: You are walking along a long, straight road, with a knapsack on your back. Ahead of you is a crossroads. As you approach it you hear the sound of castanets and, in the distance, a foghorn. An old, brown farm waggon rumbles past you. In the back of the waggon sits a large cat. In the distance, across the fields, you can see a large forest. So does this all mean anything?

Start out by examining the dream for any personal symbolism. Suppose you have a particularly strong association with cats. You always had a cat, or kitten, as a child and really love them. To you they represent love and affection, therefore you should focus on this personal interpretation rather than the universal symbolism interpretation given above.

The main points of the dream that need to be looked at are:

KNAPSACK Need to get away and be alone.

ROAD Things come easily to you.

CROSSROADS A decision.

CASTANETS Minor irritations.

FOGHORN Troubled times coming.

WAGGON Separation from loved one.

CAT Love and affection (personal symbolism).

FOREST Peace and tranquillity.

Interpreting, we can say that until now things have come fairly easily to you (*long, straight road*) but that there are now some minor irritations (*castanets*) entering the picture. These could develop into troubled times for you (*foghorn*). You need to get away and be by yourself for a while (*knapsack*) even though this will mean separating yourself from your loved one (*waggon*). You need to get down to the roots of your problem (*the waggon was brown*). Despite all this, peace and tranquillity are obtainable (*forest in the distance*).

Okay, but where does the cat come into it? Well, it is riding in the waggon, which itself represents separation from the loved one. Since the cat symbolizes love and affection we can say that, by extension, the cat is there as a representation of your loved one.

So, to simplify your dream, you have had a nice smooth time up until now but there are troubles ahead. To get over them you need to track them down to their roots. You need time alone to do this. But don't despair, you will come through it all okay.

You can see, then, that what seems like a nice ordinary dream is, in reality, a warning of things to come. Why else would you have the dream unless it were to tell you something? You'll find that, similarly, there is a reason for all dreams. They are not simply "nighttime movies" for your entertainment!

5
Lucid Dreaming

I have spoken of situations in which you realize that you are dreaming *during a dream*. This is known as *lucid* dreaming. It is not uncommon and can vary from a simple thought, "This is only a dream," to incredible freedom from all restrictions and the seeming ability to do whatever you want. Usually, in lucid dreaming, you feel certain that you are awake and then you suddenly get some kind of a clue, in the dream, that in fact you are not awake.

For example, a Gypsy I spoke with in Nottingham, England told me of waking one morning and, believing that he was wide awake, getting up out of bed and getting dressed. He and his wife then went out to their car. As they got into the car he noticed that there was a wide river running past the back of his house—and yet he knew there was no river within miles of where he lived! He said to his wife, "Look at that river. That must mean I'm dreaming." She replied that he was ridiculous. She couldn't explain the river but said they had to be wide awake. In true Romani fashion he was determined to prove that he was dreaming . . . he started the car, swung around the house, and drove into the river! As the car hit the water he woke up, still in bed.

When you experience something like this, where you realize that you are dreaming, you can sometimes go ahead and *direct* your dream; you can determine what you want to dream. But you must remain constantly alert. You need to keep reminding yourself that you are dreaming and that, therefore, you can do anything you like. Otherwise you will slip off back into the unconscious dream state and lose control.

Many dreamers enter the lucid area through nightmares. You might have a bad nightmare, something that is really frightening you. You suddenly say to yourself, in the dream, "This is ridiculous! This is only a dream. I don't need to be afraid." When most people do this they either wake up or else the nightmare retreats into a normal, non-frightening, dream. What you should do is *direct* the dream at that point; take yourself away from the nightmare aspect and move yourself on to something that you would enjoy. Incidentally, dream researchers have found that lucid dreams are more easily experienced in the hours just prior to waking in the morning.

Frederik van Eeden, a Dutch psychotherapist, reported in *A Study of Dreams* (1913):

"I dreamt that I stood at a table before a window. On the table were different objects. I was perfectly well aware that I was dreaming and I considered what sorts of experiments I could make. I began by trying to break glass, by beating it with a stone. I put a small tablet of glass on two stones and struck it with another stone. Yet it would not break. Then I took a fine claret-glass from the table and struck it with my fist, with all my might, at the same time reflecting how dangerous it would be to do this in waking life; yet the glass remained whole. But lo! when I looked at it again after some time, it was broken. It broke all right, but a little too late, like an actor who misses his cue. This gave me a very curious impression of being in a *fake world*, cleverly imitated, but with small failures.

"I took the broken glass and threw it out of the window, in order to observe whether I could hear the *tinkling*. I heard the noise all right and I even saw two dogs run away from it quite naturally. I thought what a good imitation this comedy-world was. Then I saw a decanter with claret and tasted it, and noted with perfect clearness of mind: 'Well, we can also have voluntary impressions of taste in this dream world; this has quite the taste of wine.' "

Many people who experience lucid dreaming report that such dreams are very easily remembered on waking; much more so than any other dreams.

One of the fun aspects of lucid dreaming is to be able to meet with friends, at a predetermined place, in your dreams. In fact there are various study groups around the country who "meet" on a regular basis as part of their exercises in dream investigation. In *Astral Projection* (University Books, 1962) Oliver Fox relates how he and two friends, Elkington and Slade, once spent an enjoyable evening together discussing dreams and then agreed to meet on Southampton Common in their dreams that night. Fox himself had no trouble going to the common in his dream, and became aware of meeting Elkington there. In the dream both he and Elkington commented on the fact that Slade had not shown up.

The following morning Fox met with both men. Elkington reported the same dream that Fox had experienced. But Slade complained that he considered the experiment a failure; he hadn't dreamed at all—explaining why Fox and Elkington hadn't encountered him on the Common.

6
Prophetic Dreams

" . . . when our ordinary waking consciousness or *will* goes to sleep or rest, or even dozes, that instant an entirely different power takes command of the myriad forces of memory, and proceeds to make them act, wheel, evolute, and perform dramatic tricks, such as the Common Sense of our daily life would never admit.

"This power we call the Dream, but it is more than that. It can do more than make *Us*, or *Me*, or the Waking Will, believe that we are passing through fantastic scenes. It can remember or revive the memory of things forgotten by *us*; it can, when *he* is making no effort, solve for the geometrician problems which are far beyond his waking capacity—it sometimes teaches the musician airs such as he could not compose. That is to say, within ourself (*sic*) there dwells a more mysterious Me, in some respects a more gifted Self. There is not the least reason, in the present state of Science, to assume that this is either a 'spiritual' being or an act of material forces ... This power, therefore, knows things hidden from Me, and can do what *I* cannot. Let no one incautiously exclaim here that what this really means is, that I possess higher accomplishments which I do not use. The power often actually acts against Me—it plays at fast and loose with me—it tries to deceive me, and when it finds that in dreams I have detected a blunder in the plot of the play which it is spinning, it brings the whole abruptly to an end with the convulsion of a nightmare, or by letting the *curtain* fall with a crash, and—I am awake! And then 'how the phantoms flee—how the dreams depart!' as Westwood writes. With what wonderful speed all is washed away clean from the blackboard! Our waking visions do not fly like this. But—be it noted, for it is positively true—the evanescence of our dream is, in a vast majority of instances, exactly in proportion to their folly."

Charles Godfrey Leland
Gypsy Sorcery and Fortune Telling (1891)

"This power, therefore, knows things hidden from me," says Leland. It certainly seems to. In many cases they are things that are not literally *unknown* to us, simply "hidden." Yet there have been a number of recorded cases where things revealed to a dreamer very definitely *were* totally unknown. An early example is the case of an old tinker, named John Chapman. Other than the fact that he was not nomadic, Chapman's lifestyle was pretty much like that of a Gypsy. He was a tinker-peddler living in the village of Swaffham, in the county of Norfolk, England, in the fifteenth century. He scraped a living mending pots and pans and selling odds and ends.

One night John Chapman had a strange dream. He dreamed that he was told to go to London and stand on London Bridge, where he would meet with a certain man who would bring him news of a fortune that he could have. When John told his neighbors of the dream they laughed at him. But he was very moved by it. He felt he should go, though it was over a hundred miles to London and he had no horse to take him there. His neighbors told him to forget the dream but he decided otherwise. Chapman set out for London on foot.

In those days London Bridge was a crowded, bustling span across the river

Thames. The whole bridge was covered with buildings; houses and shops. John Chapman stood in the middle of the bridge and waited.

Nothing happened. He waited there for three days, but no man appeared to him. He was loathe to go back home, knowing he would be a laughingstock. On the morning of the fourth day a shopkeeper, opposite whose shop Chapman stood, went up to him and asked what he was waiting for. Chapman told him the story, though he did not give his name nor say from where he came. The shopkeeper heard him out then laughed uproariously.

"You're a fool!" he said. "Why I had a strange dream myself, a few nights ago, but I didn't go chasing across the country because of it." Chapman asked what the dream was about. "Why," said the shopkeeper, "I dreamed of a little village in Norfolk called Swaffham, and of a man who dwelt there named John Chapman. In the dream he was a peddler and he had a pear tree in his back garden beneath which was buried a great store of treasure. Now, suppose I had gone all the way to Norfolk to dig under that tree? What a fool I'd be!" He laughed louder and louder, then returned to his store.

John Chapman lost no time in returning home. He made straight for the old pear tree in his back garden and dug down between its roots. There he found a vast fortune in gold and silver. In gratitude, Chapman gave much money to the village church. Indeed, today you can go to the church and see a wooden carving of the peddler on one of the pews, along with many stained glass windows depicting the story of his dream.

Such stories are not uncommon. Many people, in their dreams, learn things of which they had no previous knowledge whatsoever. Another famous example was the case of Maria Marten.

In 1827 Maria Marten, daughter of a couple living in Suffolk County, England, ran away with her lover William Corder, a farmer. The parents heard nothing from Maria for a long time but finally got a letter from Corder saying that he and Maria had married and that their daughter was fine. This set their minds at rest, though they never heard a word from Maria herself. One night, about a year after Corder's letter, Maria's mother had a dream. In it she saw Corder murder Maria and hide her body under the floor of a large red barn. The dream was so vivid that the Martens journeyed to the Corder farm and there Mr. Marten tore up the floorboards of the barn. The rotting body of Maria was found buried in a sack. William Corder was charged with her murder, confessed, and finally was hanged for it.

A more recent example occurred—again in Britain, in the little Welsh village of Aberfan—on the night of October 20, 1966. A little Welsh girl named Eryl Jones, nine years old, had a dream that there was no school the following day. Not just that there were no classes held, but that the school itself had disappeared. She told her mother, on the morning of the 21st, that "something black came down all over it." But she went off to school anyway. Shortly after nine o'clock that morning a half million ton mountain of coal waste, saturated by days of unrelenting rain, slid down over the village, burying houses and the entire school. Nearly one hundred fifty people—most of them schoolchildren—died.

Many other people in Britain had similar dreams of this coming disaster. In Plymouth, on England's south coast, a psychic "saw" the avalanche of coal slag pour down the mountainside onto the village. She saw many details, later verified, of the ensuing rescue attempts. One man who had never heard of the town dreamed of the word *Aberfan*. Any number had the connection of coal and Wales. There were so many reports of detailed dreams prior to the tragedy that a survey was conducted. At least thirty-six prophetic dreams could be confirmed. As a direct result of this the British Premonitions Bureau and the (New York) Central Premonitions Registry were established.

7
Dreaming for Profit

A few years ago, in 1978, a report came in to a British police station that a section of the main A-1 highway had been blocked off. Rushing out to investigate, the "bobbies" found that a group of Gypsies was responsible. There had been an argument between two Rom men over the merits of their respective horses. Finally the men had decided to race one another, to see which horse was faster. What better place to race, they thought, than down the main highway? So they blocked off a seven-mile stretch with their vardos and had their race! A Nottingham newspaper reported the event as follows:

GYPSIES SEAL OFF PART OF Al FOR DAWN HORSE RACE

Police in Notinghamshire are looking into complaints that Gypsies shut off seven miles of the Great North Road with their vehicles and turned it into a racecourse.

Villagers alongside the A1 between Sutton-on-Trent and Tuxford said yesterday that 250 Gypsies, some from as far away as Scotland, closed the road for 20 minutes while two Gypsy families decided which of them owned the best horse. One family was from Surrey and one from Doncaster. Each staked 2,000 pounds on the race along the A1. Side bets totaled several thousand pounds.

The race, run at 6 a.m., on Sunday last week, was won by the northern horse, which completed the course in 19 minutes. After the race the winning owner rejected an offer of 3,500 pounds for it.

Police in the town of Retford, near by, said: "We did not know it was happening and we are looking into it. No one has the right to close a trunk road, certainly not for horse racing." But inquiries were difficult because the gypsies left the district after the race.

The horse (not the dog) is considered by the Rom as "man's best friend." Gypsy horse dealers are the most knowledgeable anywhere in the world. Being so appreciative of horses, Gypsies—men and women—very much enjoy horse racing and, with their knowledge, usually do very well betting on races.

Some Gypsies in Kent told me of a man (a *gaujo*) they used to know who *dreamed* of horserace winners. I did some research and found that this appears to be true. The man lived in London and his name was Harold Horwood. He was an electrical engineer and his wins had been documented and verified by the London newspaper *Sunday Pictorial*. Horwood consistently won a great deal of money over a period of several years, placing bets according to his dreams. He said that on one occasion "the name of the winner was shouted at me (in the dream) so loudly that it woke me up!" The exciting thing about this is that Horwood claimed that anyone can learn his technique. Indeed, in later years his wife also started dreaming winners. Several of the Gypsies to whom I spoke tried it and they too had success.

For many years Horwood had been interested in spirit communication then later developed an interest in prophetic dreams. After a couple of tentative tries he woke up one morning, in 1945, with a word that sounded like "Sehoney" ringing in his ears. The Cambridgeshire race was soon to be run and, in looking through the list of runners, Horwood saw a horse named *Sayani*. Since the name was so similar, he backed it for a modest five pounds. He received two hundred pounds when it won.

Inspired by this he concentrated on the Manchester November Handicap, and dreamed of flashing letters "L.V.G." Looking down the runners, he backed *Las Vegas* with forty pounds and walked away with eight hundred. There were twenty-three runners in that race and the horse won at odds of 20-1. So, in just two races, Horwood won 1,000 pounds (a U.S. equivalency of about $2,500).

Symbolism often came into discovering the winners. In April of 1947 Horwood dreamed about a pride of lions playing together, with one lioness amongst them. The next day *Lion Lass* won a race. On the eve of the 1948 Cesarewitch he dreamed he was on the deck of a ship when a log of wood burst into bright flame. He stamped it out but it burst alight a second time. Again he stamped it out, but once more it happened and he kept putting out the flaming log for the rest of the night! The next day he had some hesitation when he found one horse racing named *Woodburn* and another named *Sea Smoke*. However, he didn't remember noticing any smoke in the dream so he bet on *Woodburn*. It won at 100-9.

A dream of "Mallory Marshes" translated to *Marshmallow*, another winner. Just before the 1949 Derby he remembered dreaming of a six-letter word with two syllables. He couldn't recall the word exactly but knew it was a not-too-uncommon word. *Nimbus* won at 7-1. The only other names with six letters and two syllables were *Tangui* and *Xermes*—decidedly unusual names. For the 1952 Derby he got the name clearly: *Tulyar*. It won at 11-2. So it went on, year after year.

The Society for Psychical Research learned of Horwood's precognition and examined the records. They claimed that they were "far and away the best we have received in this direction" (June 9, 1958). The Society referred him to a "team" of dreamers, the members of which all concentrated on one particular race then sent record of their dreams to the team captain for interpretation. In this way it was possible to really pinpoint a horse. However, after a time of working with the team, Horwood came to the conclusion that the best person to interpret a dream is the dreamer him or herself (due to the personal symbolism I have mentioned) and returned to working alone.

Horwood's account of the 1958 Ascot Stakes is interesting: "Concentrated on this race. Dreamed that *Secretary* would win. This was subsequently amplified by a statement (in my dream) that the winner was the secretary to the manager or owner or someone like that. Of the horses running there were none named *Secretary* but *Sandiacre* was the only horse beginning with 'S.' It also had the same number of letters as 'Secretary.' I backed it and it won at 100-7. A very interesting and instructive thing occurred the following morning when reading the story of the race. The *Daily Mail* had printed, in 1/2-inch type, '*Sandiacre* was *willed* to win' and made a prominent point of the fact that Mary Dutton, the *secretary* of the trainer, had willed the horse to win by running with it and cheering it until it passed the post."

There seems to be no consistency in the manner in which the winners are indicated in dreams. Horwood's wife had a dream prior to The Oaks, in June 1958. She told her husband how she had dreamed that a ball got into her room but every time she tried to throw it out, it would not leave her hand. She said to her husband "If only there was a horse named Tantalizer—the dream was so tantalizing." He checked and found that there *was* a horse named *Tantalizer* running in The Oaks. He bet on it. It lost! The race was won by *Bella Paola*. Horwood later said "This shows you should stick to strict interpretation of the dream, not what someone says about the dream." The ball was *Bella*; Horwood's wife's name was Pauline . . . *Bella Paola*.

On the morning of the Fenwolf Stakes, that same year, Horwood woke up with the words "Can't tell you" on his lips. He didn't know why and couldn't remember any dream. But on checking the runners he found *Cantelo*. He backed it and it won at 7-4. Examples go on and on, over many years. Sometimes the name itself is dreamed, or a close approximation; sometimes the initial(s); sometimes a number relating to the number of letters in the name; sometimes it is purely symbolic.

Another way of finding the winner, says Horwood, is over a period of time, by a process of elimination. Start by putting all the names in boxes. For example, suppose there are sixteen names. It will require four dreams to narrow down to the winner. Let's call the horses Jack, Tom, Dick, Harry, Paul, John, Jim, Sam, Ann, Gertrude, Fanny, Ethel, May, Fay, Babe, and Lil. The first day put half in one box and half in another:

LEFT BOX	RIGHT BOX
Jack	Ann
Tom	Gertrude
Dick	Fanny
Harry	Ethel
Paul	May
John	Fay
Jim	Babe
Sam	Lil

Have that list beside your bed when you go to sleep. Tell yourself that you will dream of the winner.

The next day rearrange the names so that the first and last four go in the Left Box and the second and third four go in the Right Box:

LEFT	RIGHT
Jack	Paul
Tom	John
Dick	Jim
Harry	Sam
May	Ann
Fay	Gertrude
Babe	Fanny
Lil	Ethel

Again, go to sleep with this on the bedside table and the thought that you will dream of the winner.

For the third night, make out the list with alternate pairs, left and right:

LEFT	RIGHT
Jack	Dick
Tom	Harry
Paul	Jim
John	Sam
Ann	Fanny
Gertrude	Ethel
May	Babe
Fay	Lil

For the fourth, and final, night put them alternately in the boxes:

LEFT	RIGHT
Jack	Tom
Dick	Harry
Paul	John
Jim	Sam
Ann	Gertrude
Fanny	Ethel
May	Fay
Babe	Lil

Here is a review of these listings, perhaps making them easier to understand:

Horse	Number	1st List	2nd List	3rd List	4th List
JACK	1	L	L	L	L
TOM	2	L	L	L	R
DICK	3	L	L	R	L
HARRY	4	L	L	R	R
PAUL	5	L	R	L	L
JOHN	6	L	R	L	R
JIM	7	L	R	R	L
SAM	8	L	R	R	R
ANN	9	R	R	L	L
GERTRUDE	10	R	R	L	R
FANNY	11	R	R	R	L
ETHEL	12	R	R	R	R
MAY	13	R	L	L	L
FAY	14	R	L	L	R
BABE	15	R	L	R	L
LIL	16	R	L	R	R

Now if, as a result of analyzing your dreams over the four days, you find that the first day gave you Left, the second Left, the third Right, and the fourth Left, then the only horse that corresponds to that pattern is Dick, as can be seen in the above table. This horse might also be underscored by other indications in the dream.

Another way of working, that doesn't necessarily call for a lot of dreams over several nights, is to put the names into a number of boxes before you go to sleep at night:

JACK	TOM
DICK	HARRY
PAUL	JOHN
JIM	SAM
ANN	GERTRUDE
FANNY	ETHEL
MAY	FAY
BABE	LIL

Horwood used this method quite a lot. For example, he might dream of filling his car with gas and seeing the needle of the gas gauge point to the top right, while the attendant said "Hurry up. Hurry up.'" This would indicate the top right box and the name

Harry. Another time, using this method, Horwood saw a young woman come out of a room into a passageway with doors on either side. The door she emerged from was the first on the left, and she carried a baby in her arms. This obviously indicates the horse *Babe* in the bottom left box.

Whichever method you use, says Horwood, two things are essential. One is to tell your unconscious mind, emphatically, just before you go to sleep, that you *will* dream of the winner. The other is to have pencil and paper beside the bed so that you can write down everything you remember *as soon as you wake up*. You should keep a flashlight there also, in case you wake up in the middle of the night. The Gypsies I originally spoke to about this also emphasized these two essentials. They said that Horwood's methods worked for them. They could work for you, too.

Summary

1. Start out with at least some degree of expectation that you will be successful. In other words, think positive.

2. Have a writing pad and pencil beside the bed, plus a small flashlight. I would even recommend sharpening the pencil at both ends and attaching it to the notebook with a

piece of string, so you don't lose it as you grope for it.

3. Decide on a race about a week ahead of time. Start with races that have smaller fields (numbers of horses).

4. List the runners' names in any order, preferably haphazard, so that you aren't swayed by those at the top of the list. Number them 1, 2, 3, etc., and make a Left and a Right column, as described earlier.

5. Keep the list at the side of the bed and read it all the way through several times before going to sleep. There's no need to try to memorize it. The Gypsies suggest reading it through seven times in all.

6. Say to yourself—out loud if you wish—at least three times, "I want to know which horse is going to win." If you are using the Left/Right column method, over the four days, add: "I want to know whether it is in the left or the right column."

7. Write down all you can remember *as soon as you become conscious*. Don't expect to dream of a horse race; you seldom, if ever, do. You will get the name by clues, initials, numbers, symbols, etc.

8. Don't be discouraged if you don't remember your dreams. Keep trying. It can sometimes take weeks, months, or more, so don't be discouraged.

The world of dreams can be as fascinating as the world of the Gypsies. Through your dreams you can learn more about yourself; you can learn of your past, present, and future; you can even dream for profit. Dreaming and dream interpretation can be lots of fun, enlightening and educational . . . all at no cost to you!

Happy dreams!

Kushti bok
Raymond Buckland

STAY IN TOUCH

On the following pages you will find listed, with their current prices, some of the books and tapes now available on related subjects. Your book dealer stocks most of these, and will stock new titles in the Llewellyn series as they become available. We urge your patronage.

To obtain a FREE COPY of our latest full CATALOG of New Age books, tapes, videos, crystals, products and services, just write to the address below. In each 80-page catalog sent out bimonthly, you will find articles, reviews, the latest information on New Age topics, a listing of news and events, and much more. It is an exciting and informative way to stay in touch with the New Age and the world. The first copy will be sent free of charge and you will continue receiving copies as long as you are an active customer. You may also subscribe to *The Llewellyn New Times* by sending a $2.00 donation ($7.00 for Canada & Mexico, and $20.00 for overseas). Order your copy of *The Llewellyn New Times* today!

The Llewellyn New Times
P.O. Box 64383-Dept. 086, St. Paul, MN 55164

TO ORDER BOOKS AND PRODUCTS
ON THE FOLLOWING PAGES:

If your book dealer does not carry the titles and products listed on the following pages, you may order them directly from Llewellyn. Please send full price in U.S. funds, plus $2.00 for postage and handling for the first book, and 50¢ for each additional book. There are no postage and handling charges for orders over $50. UPS Delivery: We ship UPS whenever possible. Delivery guaranteed. Provide your street address as UPS does not deliver to P.O. Boxes. UPS to Canada requires a $50 minimum order. Allow 4-6 weeks for delivery. Orders outside the U.S.A. and Canada: Airmail—add retail price of book; add $5 for each non-book item (tapes, etc.); add $1 per item for surface mail. You may use your major credit card to order these titles by calling 1-800-THE-MOON, M-F, 8:00-5:00, Central Time. Send orders to:

LLEWELLYN PUBLICATIONS
P.O. Box 64383-Dept. 086
St.Paul, MN 55164, U.S.A.

SECRETS OF GYPSY FORTUNETELLING
by Raymond Buckland, Ph. D.

This book unveils the Romani secrets of fortunetelling, explaining in detail the many different methods used by these nomads. Here you will learn to read palms, to interpret the symbols in a teacup, to read cards (both the Tarot and regular playing cards). Here are revealed the secrets of interpreting the actions of animals, of reading the weather, of recognizing birthmarks and the shape of hands.

The methods of divination presented in this book are all practical methods—no expensive or hard-to-get items are necessary. The Gypsies are accomplished at using natural objects and everyday items to serve them in their endeavors. Sticks and stones, knives and needles, cards and dice . . . some are found along the roadside, or in the woods, others are easily attainable at little expense from the five-and-dime, the convenience store, or the traveling peddler. Using these non-complex objects, and following the traditional Gypsy ways shown, you can become a seer and improve the quality of your own life and the lives of those around you.

0-87542-051-6, mass market, 240 pgs., illus.   **$3.95**

THE BUCKLAND GYPSY FORTUNETELLING DECK
by Raymond Buckland, Ph. D.

The Buckland Gypsy Fortunetelling Deck is a deck of 74 cards consisting of 22 Major Arcana and 52 Minor Arcana. They are very different from the Tarot, and are a fascinating, effective tool for divination. Created by Ray Buckland, himself a Gypsy, they are authentic and realistic.

Over the past 200 years some Romani families have designed their own Major Arcana to be used with a regular deck. These new cards often bore no resemblance to the Major Arcana of the Tarot, and even varied greatly from one Gypsy family to the next.

One such Romani deck is that of the Buckland family, presented here for the first time ever. *The Buckland Gypsy Fortunetelling Deck* is complete. Included with the deck is a 36-page instruction book that provides all necessary information needed to use the cards. The booklet contains an introduction to the deck, the meaning of each card, the names of each Major Arcana card, and several original divinatory spreads.

0-87542-052-4, 74 cards, booklet   **$12.95**

PRACTICAL COLOR MAGICK
by Raymond Buckland, Ph. D.

The world is a rainbow of color, a symphony of vibration. We have left the Newtonian idea of the world made of large mechanical units, and now know it as a strange chaos of vibrations ordered by our senses, but, our senses are limited and designed by Nature to give us access to only those vibratory emanations we need for survival.

- Learn the secret meanings of color
- Use color to change the energy centers of your body
- Heal yourself and others through light radiation
- Discover the hidden aspects of your personality through color

This book will teach all the powers of light and more! You'll learn new forms of expression of your innermost self, new ways of relating to others with the secret languages of light and color. Put true color back into your life with the rich spectrum of ideas and practical magical formulas from *Practical Color Magick*!

0-87542-047-6, 160 pgs., 5 1/4 x 8, illus., softcover $6.95

PRACTICAL CANDLEBURNING RITUALS
by Raymond Buckland, Ph. D.

Another book in Llewellyn's Practical Magick series. Magick is a way in which to apply the full range of your hidden psychic powers to the problems we all face in daily life. We know that normally we use only 5% of our total powers—Magick taps powers from deep inside our psyche where we are in contact with the Universe's limitless resources.

Magick need not be complex—it can be as simple as using a few candles to focus your mind, a simple ritual to give direction to your desire, a few words to give expression to your wish.

This book shows you how easy it can be. Here is Magick for fun, Magick as a craft, Magick for success, love, luck, money, marriage, healing; Magick to stop slander, to learn truth, to heal an unhappy marriage, to overcome a bad habit, to break up a love affair, etc.

Magick—with nothing fancier than ordinary candles, and the 28 rituals in this book (given in both Christian and Old Religion versions)—can transform your life.

0-87542-048-06, 200 pgs., 5 1/4 x 8, illus., softcover $6.95

BUCKLAND'S COMPLETE BOOK OF WITCHCRAFT
by Raymond Buckland, Ph. D.

Here is the most complete resource for the study and practice of modern, non-denominational Wicca. This is a lavishly illustrated, self-study course for a solitary practitioner or group. Included are rituals, exercises for developing psychic talents, and information on all major "sects" of the Craft, sections on tools, beliefs, dreams, meditations, divination, herbal lore, healing, ritual clothing and much more. *Buckland's Complete Book of Witchcraft* unites theory and practice into a comprehensive course designed to help you develop into a practicing Witch, one of the "Wise Ones." Written by Dr. Raymond Buckland, a well-known and respected authority on witchcraft, this book contains workbook-type exercises, profusely illustrated and full of music and chants.

Never before has so much information on "the Craft of the Wise" been collected in one place. It takes you from A to Z in the study of Witchcraft. If you want to become a Witch, or if you merely want to find out what Witchcraft is really about, you will find no better book than this.

0-87542-050-8, 272 pgs., 8 1/2 x 11, illus., softcover $12.95

WITCHCRAFT: YESTERDAY & TODAY
by Raymond Buckland, Ph. D.

This is a new video by recognized witchcraft authority Raymond Buckland, whose purpose is to straighten out the popular misconceptions about the Wiccan religion. For the approximately 70,000 to 75,000 people in the United States who consider themselves Wiccans or Pagans, this is the only completely factual "how-to" depiction of the rites and practices of their religion in the world.

This video details the origins and history of witchcraft, and discusses the resurgence of Wicca in our own day. Wiccan priests and priestesses dramatize the ancient rites and rituals. For the merely curious, there is no better way to experience the inner beauty and strength of the Craft of the Wise than from seeing a teacher in action. For students, this is better than a book; and it makes an excellent tool for coven leaders and teachers.

0-87542-089-3, VHS, approx. 60 min. $29.95

SECRETS OF GYPSY LOVE MAGICK
by Raymond Buckland, Ph. D.
For centuries the Gypsies have traveled all over the world collecting and dispensing magickal knowledge. In *Secrets of Gypsy Love Magick* you will find a collection of love spells and magick formulas that are time-tested and reliable, taken from a long tradition of successful Gypsy practice.

- Discover your future spouse
- Attract a lover
- Bring you and your lover closer together
- Keep a spouse faithful
- Retain youthful beauty and virility
- Make love potions, amulets and talismans

Gypsy magick is both positive and practical—it can be followed using ordinary, easily obtained materials.

Don't wait any longer! Bring some Gypsy love magick into your life today!

0-87542-053-2, 174 pgs., mass market, illus. $3.95

DREAMS & WHAT THEY MEAN TO YOU
by Migene Gonzalez-Wippler
Everyone dreams. Yet dreams are rarely taken seriously—they seem to be only a bizarre series of amusing or disturbing images that the mind creates for no particular purpose. Through a language of their own, however, dreams contain essential information which, if properly analyzed and understood, can change your life. In this fascinating, well-written book Migene Gonzalez-Wippler gives you all of the information needed to begin interpreting—even creating—your own dreams.

Dreams & What They Mean To You begins by exploring the nature of the human mind and consciousness, then discusses the results of the most recent scientific research on sleep and dreams. The author analyzes different types of dreams—telepathic, nightmares, sexual and prophetic. There is also an extensive dream dictionary which lists the meanings for a wide variety of dream images.

Most importantly, Gonzalez-Wippler tells you how to practice "creative dreaming"—consciously controlling dreams as you sleep. Once you learn to control your dreams, your horizons will expand and your chances of success will increase a hundredfold!

0-87542-288-8, 240 pgs., mass market $3.95

WHAT YOUR DREAMS CAN TEACH YOU
by Alex Lukeman

Dreams have much to teach us, but the lessons are often difficult to comprehend. Confusion comes not from the dream but from the outer mind's attempt to understand it.

What Your Dreams Can Teach You is a workbook of self-discovery, a systematic and proven approach to the understanding of dreams. It does *not* contain lists of meanings for dream symbols. Only you, the dreamer, can discover what the images in your dreams mean for you. The book *does* contain step-by-step information which can lead you to success with your dreams, success that will bear fruit in your waking hours. Learn to tap into the aspect of yourself that truly knows how to interpret dreams, the inner energy of the "Dreamer Within." This aspect of your consciousness will lead you to an accurate understanding of your dreams and even assist you in interpreting the dreams of others.

0-87542-475-9, 288pgs., 6 x 9, illus.   **$12.95**

HOW TO DREAM YOUR LUCKY LOTTO NUMBERS
by Raoul Maltagliati

Until now, there has been no scientific way to predict lotto numbers . . . they come up by chance. But overnight, you may find them through a trip into the dimension of the collective unconscious, where "time" and "chance," as we know them, do not exist. In *How to Dream Your Lucky Lotto Numbers,* you will be introduced to an actual dream interpreter, who will guide you in picking your lucky lotto numbers! Author Raoul Maltagliati explains:

- Why we dream
- How to isolate the key points in a dream that indicate your lotto numbers
- How to find the numeric equivalents of dream subjects
- How to keep your lotto numbers within the parameters of your lottery (between 1 and 56, for example)
- How to adjust for the Moon's influence on your dreams
- The importance of the day and the month during which you have your lotto dreams

An extensive dream dictionary helps you discover what numbers you should pick based on your most recent dreams.

0-87542-483-X, 112 pgs., mass market   **$3.95**